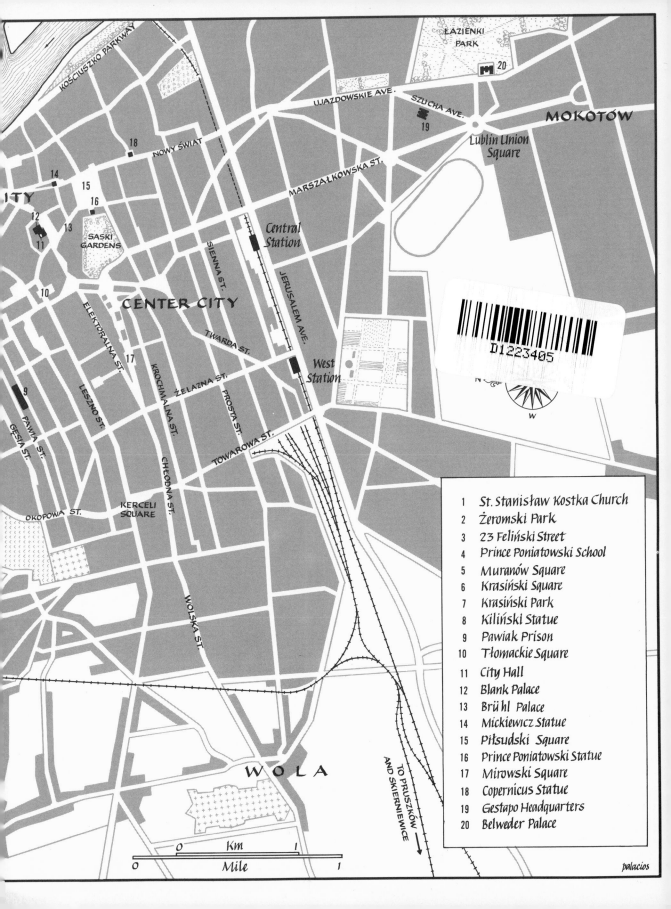

DYING, WE LIVE

I. VIII. 06   WASZYNGTON

The author, age fourteen, in uniform of Fire Brigade Cadet-Officer, 1944

Julian Eugeniusz Kulski

DYING, WE LIVE

*The Personal Chronicle of
a Young Freedom Fighter
in Warsaw (1939–1945)*

Holt, Rinehart and Winston
New York

Copyright © 1979 by Julian Eugeniusz Kulski

Published by
Holt, Rinehart and Winston,
383 Madison Avenue, New York,
New York 10017.

Published simultaneously in Canada
by Holt, Rinehart and Winston of Canada, Limited.

Library of Congress Cataloging in Publication Data

Kulski, Julian Eugene, 1929–
    Dying, we live.

    1.   World War, 1939–1945—Poland—Warsaw—Biography—
Underground movements.   2.   World War, 1939–1945—Personal
narratives, Polish.   3.   Kulski, Julian Eugene, 1929–
4.   Warsaw—Biography.   5.   Soldiers—Poland—Biography.
6.   Poland.   Polskie Siły Zbrojne.   Armia Krajowa—
Biography.   I.   Title.
D802.P62W36 1979   940.53′438′4 [B]   78-31656

ISBN: 0-03-040901-2

First Edition

Printed in the United States of America
10 9 8 7 6 5 4 3 2 1

*A list of illustration credits
will be found on page 304.*

TO MY COMRADES-IN-ARMS,
THE NINTH COMPANY COMMANDOS

I was ever a fighter, so—one fight more,
    The best and the last!
I would hate that death bandaged my eyes, and
       forbore,
And bade me creep past.

ROBERT BROWNING

Before I believe in my country's death,
. . . . ,
I shall first put her on the wings
Of my song,
and fly her towards Heaven and God.

JULIUSZ SŁOWACKI

FOREWORD

The Ninth Company Commandos existed for some time before the 1944 Warsaw Uprising, with small units taking part in various hard-fought battles. But from the very first day of the Uprising, the Company started to operate in full strength as an independent unit.

Without any doubt this Company was the best unit in the Żoliborz Division. It was most effective in its close contact surprise attacks on the enemy. Used in special actions, the Company was the first in attack and the last in withdrawal.

Divided into three platoons, the whole Company was never more than one hundred and fifty strong. Sixty percent of the Company's complement were in their teens, and fifteen to twenty percent were girls. The latter took part in all activities—they served in the signals section, as nurses, as cooks, as couriers, and as front line fighters. For example, a seventeen-year-old girl was in charge of the food service, while an even younger girl was in charge of ammunition and weapons supplies and maintenance. All of these girls were very courageous, way beyond any expectations, and their conduct and heroism inspired their male comrades-in-arms.

The Company consisted entirely of volunteers, and they came from every walk of life. One platoon had many from the upper class of Żoliborz, while another was made up almost completely of volunteers from the poorest section of the Powązki area. But all the fighters were highly motivated, and ready to contribute what they could.

The soldiers did receive some training in small groups within the Underground, mostly on the theory of fighting and the use of weapons and explosives. On the first day of the Uprising, however, they were faced with the fact that the only way to survive was to learn fast or otherwise pay dearly.

There were heroic tasks performed; there was bloodshed and suffering, but surprisingly few tears.

Dying, We Live tells the truth, while also bringing a message of desperate importance: *it is difficult to obtain freedom, but it is even more difficult to maintain it.*

The author was one of the youngest of the fighters. He was lucky, he survived. But I was the luckiest of them all. I not only survived, but had the privilege to see them winning . . .

M. S. Morawski ('SZELIGA')

Commander,
The Ninth Company Commandos,
1944 Warsaw Uprising

New York, 1979

AUTHOR'S NOTE

On September 1, 1939, the Germans started World War II when they attacked Poland. I was ten and a half years old at the time.

This book is the story of my growing up in Warsaw during five long years of the German Occupation. It is based on a diary I kept then and on memoirs written in Britain in September 1945. I was sixteen years old by that time, and completed my chronicle as an attempt to put the experiences of war behind me in order to start a new life.

Most of the photographs used in this book are ones I have collected since the war, but a few are family photographs which miraculously survived the long years of destruction and upheaval.

Forty years have now elapsed since the beginning of World War II, yet it is harder than ever to fully perceive and accept the inhumanity of that wartime period. When it was suggested that my personal chronicle should be published, I saw that this should be done for one reason only—to let my experiences stand in memory of my comrades and of the countless other brave people of Warsaw who symbolize the triumph of the human spirit over oppression and terror.

JULIAN E. KULSKI

Orlean, Virginia
August 1, 1979
(The thirty-fifth anniversary of the Warsaw Uprising)

The Family

FATHER—Julian Spitosław Kulski

MOTHER—Eugenia Helena Kulska (née Solecka)

SISTER—Wanda Krystyna Kulska

UNCLE NORBERT—Norbert Barlicki (Godfather)

AUNT STACHA—Stanisława Barlicka (née Kulska), estranged wife of Uncle Norbert

UNCLE JUZEK—Józef Solecki, Mother's cousin

AUNT ZOSIA—Zofia Solecka, Mother's sister

AUNT WANDA—Wanda Wyczółkowska (Godmother)

My Friends

BASIA—Barbara Kołodziejska, Home Army nurse (Danka's twin)

'BRATEK'—Jan Rocki, fellow Commando and firefighter

DANKA—Danuta Kołodziejska, Home Army nurse (Basia's twin)

'LONGINUS'—Jan Wąsowski, fellow Commando

LUDWIK—Ludwik Berger, leader of the armed Youth Resistance Movement in Żoliborz

MARYSIA—Maria Krzywicka (girl friend)

OLA—Aleksandra Sokal, Underground courier

STEFA—Stefania Sokal, Ola's sister

'THUR'—Janusz Kiciński, fellow Commando

'WILK'—Jan Domaniewski, fellow Commando

ZULA—Suzanna Chomicka (girl friend)

Wartime Leaders

NORBERT BARLICKI—Statesman; Co-organizer of the Resistance Movement in Auschwitz

ADAM CZERNIAKÓW—Chairman of the Jewish Council, and "Mayor" of the Warsaw Ghetto

STEFAN GROT-ROWECKI ('Grabica')—General and Commander-in-Chief of the Union for Armed Resistance (ZWZ) and the Home Army (AK), 1939–1943

TADEUSZ KOMOROWSKI ('Bór')—General and Commander-in-Chief of the Home Army (AK), 1943–1945

JULIAN SPITOSŁAW KULSKI—Vice President (Deputy Mayor) of Warsaw, 1935–1939; President (Lord Mayor) of Warsaw, 1939–1944

MIECZYSŁAW NIEDZIELSKI ('Żywiciel')—Colonel and Commander, Żoliborz Home Army Units

STEFAN STARZYŃSKI—President (Lord Mayor) of Warsaw, 1934–1939

The Occupiers

LUDWIG FISCHER (SA *Gruppenführer*)—Governor of the Warsaw District, 1939–1945

HANS FRANK—Governor General of the *Generalgouvernement* of Occupied Poland, 1939–1945

FRIEDRICH WILHELM KRÜGER (SS *Obergruppenführer*)—Head of SS and Police for the *Generalgouvernement* of Occupied Poland, 1939–1943

FRANZ KUTSCHERA (SS *Brigadeführer*)—Head of SS and Police for the Warsaw District, October 1943–February 1944

LUDWIG LEIST (SA *Brigadeführer*)—*Stadthauptmann* of Occupied Warsaw, 1940–1944

JÜRGEN STROOP (SS *Brigadeführer*)—Head of SS and Police for the Warsaw District, April–September 1943; Commander-in-Chief, German Forces, Ghetto Uprising, 1943

ERICH VON DEM BACH (SS *Obergruppenführer*)—Head of the German Counterinsurgency Forces, European Theater; Commander-in-Chief, German Forces, Warsaw Uprising, 1944

DYING, WE LIVE

Blank Palace inner courtyard, as seen from City Hall

City Hall and Blank Palace (nineteenth-century)

Brühl Palace

Father—1919

Mother—1919

Author—1944 (age fourteen)

Sister—1937 (age five)

Aunt Stacha (postwar photograph)   Uncle Norbert—1918   Uncle Juzek—1919

Aunt Wanda, Mother, Aunt Jadwiga, Father—1919

Ludwik—1942

Stefa—1946

Basia—1945

'Wilk'—1944

Marysia—1944

Family photo—1939

Adam Czerniaków—1941

M. S. Morawski—1946

*Julian S. Kulski,
author's father—1947*

Stefan Starzyński—1933

Ludwig Leist (center) *and Ludwig Fischer* (to Leist's left)

Ludwig Leist

Erich von dem Bach

1939

THURSDAY, AUGUST 24

Today, Father, Mother, Wanda, and I came to Kazimierz. My father says that war is imminent, and he is anxious that we be safe. He does not know, of course, how long he will be able to stay here with us.

SATURDAY, AUGUST 26

Kazimierz is an old city on the river Vistula, famous for its marketplace, its ancient synagogue, and its historic buildings. We are staying at the Filipkowskis' boardinghouse, set amid varied and beautiful trees on a grassy hillside near the town center. Not far from our boardinghouse are small houses occupied by Orthodox Jews. Yesterday evening, Friday, the Jewish men, dressed in long black robes and skullcaps, celebrated their holiday. The rooms were lit with candles, and the men bowed as they prayed in loud voices. The Filipkowskis' son, Jędrek, and I watched them through the window, then rattled it and ran away.

SUNDAY, AUGUST 27

The weather is splendid. We have been going for walks, and swimming in the Vistula. Last night, however, a car came with a letter from City President Stefan Starzyński, the Lord Mayor of Warsaw, ordering my father to return to the capital at once. Father told us that we should stay in Kazimierz until he either returns or sends for us. I asked to go back with my father. If there is going to be a war, I do not want to miss it. Besides, my school has collected money for the defense of Poland and has contributed to a motor torpedo boat, so I feel I should be allowed to fight. Father told me that I was too young to fight, as I am only ten, and that I should look after Mother and Wanda. I pointed out to Father that boys my age had disarmed Germans on the streets of Warsaw during the World War, but he is adamant that I do as I am told. I am very disappointed.

MONDAY, AUGUST 28

Jędrek, the youngest son of Mr. Filipkowski, is eight years old. He and I put frogs in the well today so we are in trouble. My mother, with the other women, is looking after the cow, the garden, and the fields. She says it is the first time in her life that she has dug potatoes, taken a cow to pasture, and carried water from a well, but she seems to be enjoying it.

FRIDAY, SEPTEMBER 1

Today, Friday, I was in the woods picking mushrooms with a friend. A white eagle had been hovering lazily over the deep gorge, but suddenly the eagle disappeared, and we heard the sound of engines. We saw planes flying overhead, just above the treetops. They had black crosses on their wings and heavy canister-shaped objects under them. The noise they made frightened us. We ran back toward the old town at the foot of the hill, and as it was market day, we headed for the main square.

The old town square was filled with wagons, and mangy horses with fly-covered ribs. It was bursting with pigs and chickens. Peasant women in colorful babushkas perched on the wagons, selling their goods to black-clad Jews, the babble of Polish-Yiddish mixing with the cackling and squealing of the animals. We decided to leave and started our climb back up the hill past the synagogue. Halfway up I left my friend, Zula, at her house and took a back trail home through the woods.

My mother was waiting for me when I reached home. She told me that she was getting worried about what was going on in Warsaw. She had not been able to learn much from the news on the radio, and she was thinking of Father. However, this much we do know—Germany has invaded Poland, and the war has started. I have no doubts that Poland will win the war, but I am so afraid that it will be over before I have a chance to participate.

SUNDAY, SEPTEMBER 10

Today the Germans bombed the town. I was scared and asked

Mother if this was happening all over Poland, or was it just in Kazimierz. She said she had no way of knowing, and I wished that Father were here so that I could ask him. He would know the answer. Many people went to the ravines, taking food and bedding with them and spending several hours there. The synagogue caught fire.

The Invasion

FRIDAY, SEPTEMBER 15

The Germans have come in their dirty gray green uniforms and helmets, carrying rifles. They didn't appear at all as I had imagined —in fact, I wasn't impressed, but Mother doesn't share my feelings. The noise of their motorcycles on the cobblestones shook the streets. They went to the main square and placed a field gun there, while cars with loudspeakers went around the city telling the inhabitants of Kazimierz that they had been freed by the armies of the Third Reich. Then a military band played, and they raised the German flag.

German troops entering Kazimierz

THURSDAY, SEPTEMBER 21

Today Zula and her family left Kazimierz. I will miss her, but they want to get back to Warsaw.

FRIDAY, SEPTEMBER 22

Last night, after I was supposed to be asleep, I went back down-stairs. Mr. Filipkowski and some of the others were sitting around the table, busily discussing the news of the war.

We knew that some of our soldiers have been hiding in the house, and Mother asked what they would do. Mr. Filipkowski said that, in view of Russia now also having invaded Poland—from the east this time—the soldiers will have to try and get out through Hungary. Then they will attempt to rejoin their units, which are re-grouping and organizing to get back into the war. This latest news bewildered me completely. I know why the Germans are fighting us, but I wondered what the Russians had to do with it since they, like us, are traditional enemies of Germany.

SATURDAY, SEPTEMBER 23

This afternoon we heard a broadcast from Warsaw. It was Mayor Starzyński speaking:

> . . . I wanted Warsaw to be great . . . and Warsaw is great. It has happened sooner than we thought. I see her through the window in her full greatness and glory, surrounded by swirling clouds of smoke, red-dened by flames of fires, grandiose, indestructible, great Fighting Warsaw.
>
> Although where there were going to be beautiful homes, rubble now lies; although where there were going to be parks, there are today barricades, thickly covered with bodies; although our libraries are aflame —not in fifty years, not in a hundred years, but *today* Warsaw is at the height of her greatness and glory.

His words were suddenly cut short. Radio Warsaw was silent. I do hope Father is all right, and I wish I were with him in Warsaw.

SUNDAY, SEPTEMBER 24

It has turned cold so my mother has had to borrow warm clothes for us. It was summer when we came to Kazimierz, and now it is almost winter.

We are fretting and waiting. We hear on the radio that Warsaw has fallen, and we are getting more and more anxious about Father.

SUNDAY, OCTOBER 1

Father came in an official car to collect us today, and I told him I thought it was about time. But when I calmed down a bit I realized how haggard and tired he was. There were no other cars on the road except German ones, and it was an eerie—but surprisingly uneventful—ride back to Warsaw. On the way, my father told us of the surrender of Warsaw, which took place on September 28.

The fighting units entered Krasiński Square from Bonifraterska Street. With colors forward, marching along Słowacki and Mickiewicz Streets from the suburb of Bielany, wounded and unwounded alike reached the foot of the statue of Kiliński, still standing with saber in hand.

In the middle of the square, they laid down their arms. A few civilians were standing by, in tears. A colonel in full battle dress, worn but erect, entered the square. Father had a copy of the surrender speech that the colonel then made:

> Soldiers of Warsaw!
> Our misfortune is temporary.
> Victory is on our side.
> Poland is not yet lost as long as we live.
> And this which has been taken from us by force, we will take back by force.
> The country thanks you, soldiers of all ranks, for all your hardships, for your bold and unfettered stand in this heroic battle.
> Remember that we will leave this world, but the fame and memory of your deeds will live forever.

The Surrender

*Surrendered Polish Army matériel
at foot of Kiliński Statue in Krasiński
Square*

Surrendered Polish Army matériel in front of Brühl Palace

When we reached the city, we saw rubble, burned-out cars, and dead horses. Buildings still standing had empty, gaping windows. The only people on the streets were Germans, but for some reason they didn't stop our limousine.

Our house in Żoliborz has lost half its roof where a bomb fell. There is no glass in any of the windows, and the staircase is covered with dirt and slivers of glass which crunch under my feet. The furniture is in place, but dust and dead leaves have drifted into the rooms. The plants in the conservatory have withered and died, and my pets are gone. It is silent, save for the wind blowing through the rooms.

It is our house but it is different.

The Center City, late Autumn 1939

The Royal Castle, late 1939

THURSDAY, OCTOBER 5

Against my mother's orders, I went to see Zula this afternoon. As I was walking along a rubble-strewn street I noticed German soldiers and policemen evacuating almost the entire length of Ujazdowskie Avenue—not only the apartment houses on the boulevard itself, but those on the side streets as well. Men, women, and children were forced out of the buildings and marched off. They carried nothing. I noticed that the window shades were drawn in every building, and wondered what on earth was happening.

As nobody tried to stop me, I went on. When I got to Zula's building I rang the bell, wondering if she too had been marched

16

Hitler on way to Victory Parade, October 1939

off. She let me in, and we went upstairs; she told me that an hour earlier the Germans had gone up and down the streets announcing that all windows must be closed and all blinds drawn. Anyone seen either on a balcony or at a window would be shot without warning. Zula was alone, as her parents had gone to see some friends on Miła Street, so she was glad to have company.

At first, we could hear only the rumble of tank treads on the cobblestones. I cautiously moved the window shade. Rolling in perfect formation, row upon row of gleaming tanks were moving down Ujazdowskie Avenue, with black-uniformed troops standing at attention in the open hatches. There was a band playing across the street, but we could barely hear it above the noise of the tanks.

Then came the artillery, followed by goose-stepping, steel-helmeted troops in rows of twelve. I marveled at how they raised their legs with such perfect precision. The march-past of the magnificent robots continued beneath the long sinewy red flags that were suspended from the light standards on both sides of the boulevard. In the center of each flag was a white circle with a twisted black cross. Its sense of jagged movement carried with it an inexplicable feeling of fear and foreboding.

*Troops at foot of
Prince Poniatowski Statue,
Piłsudski Square,
October 1939*

*Piłsudski
Square,
with officers
saluting
the Führer,
October 1939*

Ujazdowskie Avenue, with Hitler taking salute at Victory Parade, October 1939

The band played on as the last rows passed Belweder Palace, once the home of Marshal Piłsudski. Then I remembered the military parade on Piłsudski Square on the Third of May, 1938—a glorious parade of different tanks, different colors, and different men. The magnificent horses, the yellow-capped cavalry—the Ułani, with drawn swords shining in the sun—all were missing today. The somber, Bach-like march of industrialized machines, the robotlike soldiers, conquerors of a ruined city—what a contrast to the gay music, the horses with lively tails, and the proud and smiling Ułani, with red and white guidons flying on lances above their heads.

But this was not a victory. This was a parade of Germans for Germans. It was not for us. Here in the heart of Warsaw, a place close to the heart of every Pole, the pulsating drums of an ancient enemy reached a dreadful crescendo before receding in the autumn dusk.

The center of attention was in Łazienki Park, where there was a podium with generals taking the salute. They stood behind a solitary figure whose right arm was raised at an angle. If he spoke, we could not hear him.

I had to leave Zula soon after that in order to get home before curfew. As I made my way to nearby Lublin Union Square to catch the streetcar, I felt more determined than ever that I was going to participate in this war somehow.

FRIDAY, OCTOBER 6

Today, in Berlin, Hitler made a speech. We heard it on the radio, in gloomy silence. There was a lot of boasting about victory; about how Poland had tried his patience too long; about how the Germans and Russians were going to collaborate over Poland to bring peace; about the solution to the "Jewish Problem"; and about how the Germans were going to fight and to destroy Europe if Churchill opposed him. "Yes," said my father, repeating the last words of the speech, "'Destiny will decide who is right.'"

19

THURSDAY, OCTOBER 26

Autumn leaves were drifting down from the linden trees as I made my way home along Feliński Street this evening, after taking the family dachshund for a walk. As I entered the house I could hear the voices of my father and Uncle Norbert in the study. They were somber, but Uncle Norbert gave me his usual enthusiastic hug and greeting. Then they went back to what they had been discussing.

I sat down in a corner of the room and listened, but they talked almost in whispers. Both men looked very pale. Then my father began reading aloud from the *New Warsaw Courier*, the daily paper which the Germans have now taken over. It was a proclamation by the new Governor General, Hans Frank, made from German Headquarters for Poland at Wawel Castle in Cracow:

> Polish Citizens!
>
> The Führer has ordered me as Governor General for Occupied Polish Territories to make quite sure that in the future a state of peace will be guaranteed in this country. . . .
>
> Under a just government everyone will work for his daily bread. There will, however, be no room in the territories under German rule for political provocateurs, economic jackals, and Jewish profiteers.
>
> Any attempts at resistance in the Polish territories against given regulations or law and order will be handled with utmost severity and with all the might of the powerful Great German Reich.

When he finished reading, my father was deathly silent. Uncle Norbert said only, "Every word is a crime!"

The same issue of the *New Warsaw Courier* contained two other proclamations, the first of which incensed Uncle Norbert even more than the one my father had just read. My uncle read aloud:

> One. The inhabitants of the General Government Area of Polish nationality, from eighteen to sixty years of age, immediately have the responsibility of forced labor.

Two. Only people who can prove that they are already engaged in useful work are not required to perform forced labor.

Three. Forced labor will especially be performed in agriculture, road construction, building of waterways and railroads.

Uncle Norbert continued in a tense voice:

Four. Any kind of cruelty to animals is forbidden. I therefore immediately ban ritualistic slaughter, that is, any cruel killing of animals through gradual bloodletting for the purpose of the so-called Kosher consumption of meats.

Five. Any person who commits ritualistic killing is subject to a sentence of at least one year in a maximum security prison.

Any person who is an accomplice to, or who encourages and assists, ritualistic killing is subject to the same punishment.

Serving of a sentence in a maximum security prison can also be carried out in concentration camps.

The first German propaganda poster, showing a Polish soldier pointing to the ruins of Warsaw and cursing Chamberlain, ENGLAND! THIS IS YOUR DOING!

I had kept quiet, but now I broke in to ask: "I can understand what the first part means, but not the last. Does it mean Jews will not be able to get meat to eat?"

"Exactly," said Uncle Norbert. "We are now beginning to see the first phase of the German Occupation Policy. Unfortunately, there will be more. I hate to think what will follow."

Uncle Norbert left soon afterward. A sense of gloom filled every room of the house.

FRIDAY, OCTOBER 27

Father came home upset. The Gestapo arrested Starzyński at the City Hall today, and my father is now Lord Mayor of Warsaw. Father said Starzyński tried to have his adviser, Dr. Kipa, accompany him, since he himself does not speak German. But the Germans would not allow it. I wonder what all this will mean for us.

MONDAY, OCTOBER 30

Mother is beside herself with worry. Earlier today, Father's office called to say that he had been taken to Gestapo Headquarters for questioning. In the afternoon he was brought home by two Gestapo men. They took him to the library and told him to stay there. I was playing on the living room floor with the small fleet of balsa boats that Uncle Norbert had given me. Both Gestapo men came to where I was and asked what I was doing. I said I was playing with my Polish and German boats. One was a two-foot-long destroyer, the other a small submarine. One of the Gestapo men asked me if the large boat was German.

"No, that's Polish!" I protested. They laughed and left to search the rest of the house.

TUESDAY, OCTOBER 31

Uncle Norbert has been to the house again. I was having a cup of tea in the kitchen with Aunt Stacha, but as soon as she heard Uncle Norbert's booming voice in the hallway, her teacup clattered to the floor. She escaped to her room and locked the door before Uncle caught sight of her.

Uncle Norbert asked for my father, but he was not at home. So he left a copy of the paper, pointing out to me still another of those proclamations by Hans Frank, which he said I should show to Father. He left quickly and said he would call later.

I took the paper and went to Aunt Stacha's room. Her eyes were wet, and she looked old and frail. I sat down on the end of the couch and asked if I could read the proclamation to her. She nodded, and I read:

> One. Person who commits violence against German authorities—death penalty.
>
> Two. Person who damages German installations —death penalty.
>
> Three. Person who calls for disobedience of German laws—death penalty.
>
> Four. Person who commits violence against a German because he is a German—death penalty.
>
> Five. Person who damages the property of a German—death penalty.
>
> Six. Person who attempts to commit violence against members of German forces—death penalty.
>
> Seven. Person who agrees to commit a crime— death penalty.
>
> Eight. Person who receives information about an attempted crime, . . . and fails to inform authority immediately—death penalty.
>
> Nine. Person who possesses arms, ammunition, hand grenades, explosives, or other military equipment—death penalty.
>
> Ten. Person who receives information about illegal possession of arms by another and fails to report it—death penalty.

All the time I was reading she was shaking her head, as if in disbelief. "What does it mean?" I asked.

"It means great danger and harm to us all," was her response. I can't stand it—except for Father, everyone here still treats me like a child. They won't give me proper answers to anything.

WEDNESDAY, NOVEMBER 1

A heavy snow fell last night. Winter is here. Slowly the plywood in our windows is being replaced with glass, but the house is still freezing as there is a shortage of coke, and we have to wear mittens inside. For the first time in my life, I had horse steak for dinner; it is already difficult to get food, and this worries Mother tremendously. I told her I would help, and that we would manage somehow.

FRIDAY, NOVEMBER 10

German soldiers came to our house early this morning, and without explanation they took Father with them. Mother is desperately trying to find out why he was arrested, and where he is, but no one seems to know what is going on. So we just have to wait—the hardest thing of all, especially for me.

WEDNESDAY, NOVEMBER 15

Father came back today. It seems that the Germans had heard there was to be some kind of Polish protest, and so they had taken Father and other leaders as hostages. When nothing happened, the Germans set the hostages free, but warned them that they would all be watched constantly. I asked Father to tell me what this means, but for once even he won't talk to me.

THURSDAY, NOVEMBER 16

The streets of Warsaw are still piled high with rubble, and bodies are still being discovered. Squares and parks have been turned into mass graves.

Father says the Germans are taking many high schools for army barracks. They have already requisitioned most automobiles, and all guns and radios have had to be turned in. I was really mad at losing my Philips wireless, a birthday present earlier this year, but Father told me to stop complaining and do as I was told.

FRIDAY, NOVEMBER 17

The Germans have even printed new money and new stamps, which today I spent adding to my stamp album. The Germans have taken the Polish issues and overlaid them with a German eagle and the word GENERALGOUVERNEMENT. Why have they ruined our beautiful stamps? Even those they cannot leave alone!

SATURDAY, NOVEMBER 18

Inwalidów and Wilson Squares are only a few blocks from home, and I go there to read the posters on the billboards. Whenever I see a throng of people around one of them, I know there is a new proclamation.

Today at Inwalidów Square I spotted my old Scoutmaster Ludwik Berger. He is tall and towers over the crowd so it is hard to miss him. I made my way to where he stood and greeted him. He seemed troubled. He said he has been very busy, but is going to let me know about the status of our Scout troop. He then strode off in a rush, his long coat flapping behind him as he went.

MONDAY, NOVEMBER 20

I made my way through the bombed-out section of Polish Army Avenue to get to school today. Many of the apartment houses along the boulevard are shorn cleanly and precisely, as if by a huge knife. I can look into the open rooms and see the furniture, wallpaper, and fixtures.

As I approached the school, I could see some of my classmates standing outside. A notice, SCHOOL CLOSED, was posted on the doors. What good news! We were elated, but curious, since there was no explanation. Then we saw our science teacher, Mr. Lewandowski, coming toward us. He told us that he did not know who had given the order, or why, but that all the other schools are also closed. Mr. Lewandowski said he would get in touch with us and that we should go home.

TUESDAY, NOVEMBER 21

Today I was surprised when I opened the door to find my science teacher standing there. He asked to see my mother, who told me later that I am one of those selected to continue school. Of course, my mother agreed, without consulting me, that I would go. Classes will be held secretly, in different houses and on different days. The rule is that we should go alone and not carry any books. To start with, we are to have only science with Mr. Lewandowski and history lessons from Mrs. Bernardyńska. This part may not be bad, for she gives wonderful lessons. She teaches Polish history backwards so we start with what we know. She is a tremendous patriot and fills our heads with the history of previous struggles for freedom, making the figures of past centuries come alive from the pages.

WEDNESDAY, NOVEMBER 22

Between classes I explore the city. People are starting to mend windows and clear away rubble. Most people walk everywhere because the streetcars are too crowded now that the front portion is reserved for Germans only; the streetcars are also dangerous because the Germans sometimes stop them and herd the passengers off in order to hold them as hostages, or to send them to work camps. I am beginning to realize that the fears I had in Kazimierz were unfounded. This war is not going to end quickly, and I will have plenty of time to fight. The question now is, when and how?

The streets are full of movement during the day, but at the curfew hour they are deserted and quiet except for the sound of German boots and the sirens of the police cars. That noise is becoming synonymous with fear. The searches are turning Warsaw into a city of terror.

FRIDAY, NOVEMBER 24

The Germans are posting more and more proclamations at the order of Governor General Frank, General Friedrich Wilhelm Krüger, and the new Governor of Warsaw, Ludwig Fischer. Today, the newspaper carried orders about Jews. Beginning Decem-

Seller of Star of David armbands, December 1939

27

ber 1, they are to wear on their right arm a white band with a Star of David on it. It has begun to dawn on me that the Germans are not going to treat all Poles alike. I wonder if *we* will have to wear bands with a cross (for Christians) on them?

TUESDAY, DECEMBER 5

Today we celebrated Father's forty-seventh birthday. We didn't have the usual happy gathering, of course, but we did our best. I gave him a carving I had made.

THURSDAY, DECEMBER 14

I saw Zula again today, and we read the *New Warsaw Courier*. It gave another list of orders about forced labor. Now, anybody between fourteen and sixty is subject to forced labor, but for Jews it is between twelve and sixty, and they also have to be registered. Some people are to go to work camps. Zula cried. Nearly all of her friends are over twelve so they will be affected. She will too, of course.

SATURDAY, DECEMBER 16

It is becoming more and more difficult to see Zula. Our house is filling up with relatives from all over the country so I can't invite her here, and every time I go to see her at her parents' apartment somebody new is there. Bolek, one of my friends from the Scouts, has lent me the key to a small apartment off Nowy Świat where he lives with his mother. Today I met Zula there when they were away. When I see Zula, I am elated but also disturbed. Today she was really edgy, and as soon as we entered the apartment she burst into tears. I tried to comfort her, and after a while she stopped crying and rested her head against my chest. But I couldn't get her to tell me what was troubling her so much.

MONDAY, DECEMBER 18

We are getting ready for Christmas Eve. Mother wants it to be traditional, in spite of everything. At first, I felt this was rather silly, but when I thought about it I realized that we had to keep some semblance of normality in order to maintain our morale. My sister, Wanda, and I are making different paper decorations for the Christmas tree, while Mother has bought food on the Black Market, such as fruit, nuts, and flour. She and the maids, Mary and Olesia, have baked long white Christmas loaves (some plain and some with poppy seeds), gingerbread, and spice cakes, and also my favorite dish, small ravioli with mushrooms. They throw me out of the kitchen frequently, as I help myself to these goodies.

SUNDAY, DECEMBER 24

We usually have twelve people for the Christmas Eve dinner—this year there were ten, including the relatives living in our house, and two close friends of my parents, "Uncle" and "Aunt" Ancyporowicz, who live nearby. The table was covered with a white tablecloth, spread with symbolic hay. In the middle of the table Mother put the bread and a plate with small pieces of wafer. While the women were busy cooking the dinner, Wanda and I decorated the Christmas tree in the living room. The tree is so tall that it reaches the ceiling. When we had finished, the doors to this room were then closed.

On the table there were two candelabra with six candles in each—during Christmas Eve dinner there can be no light other than candles. Everyone was wearing their best clothes, and we waited for the moment when we could begin—not until the first star is showing in the sky. I saw it and ran to the dining room, all excited. Then Mother took the plate with the wafers and, starting with our guests, we broke the wafers with each other, wishing that by the next Christmas Eve dinner the war will be over, and the Germans will be gone. In previous years I had found this ceremony a bit sloppy and embarrassing, but this year I really didn't mind, as it now made real sense to wish each other well, and it all seemed more sincere this time.

Now we could start the meal. First we had soup and ravioli, then fish, potatoes, sauerkraut salad, and stuffed cabbage with rice and mushrooms. This was followed by a compôte made from different dried fruits, and a traditional Christmas Eve supper dish, *Kutia*, made from boiled wheat and poppy seeds and honey.

After dinner we heard a bell ringing from the room where the Christmas tree is. We opened the doors, and there was the tree, lit with small candles of different colors. Under the tree were packages of various shapes and sizes. First we sung the carol "God Is Here," and then I went over to the tree; I took the packages one by one and handed them out, according to the names on the gift cards. While we were singing carols, Olesia and Mary were having their Christmas Eve dinner and Mother served them. After they finished they came to sing with us, and we had more poppy seed cake, gingerbread, nuts, and wine or honey mead. At eleven the adults went to Saint Stanisław Kostka Church, which is close to our house, for Midnight Mass and a carol service. Even the Germans permitted it this special night, but I noticed that, as always, I had to stay behind with my little sister.

1940

MONDAY, JANUARY 1

Feliński Street is under a deep blanket of snow. Our house, a big solid stucco structure built just before the war, is not fully repaired yet from the war damage, but even in winter the sunlight floods most of its rooms during the day. It still has a spacious, open, and inviting feeling about it.

The main entrance to the house is framed by silver pines. The paneled entry hall opens onto a large living room, a dining room, and a curving staircase. The staircase has a soft, red, thickly plaited rope that is suspended from the wall by shiny brass supports.

The living room, finished in soft yellow-gold, glows in the sunlight entering through a large double expanse of glass walls. Between these walls is the winter garden, with small statues hidden among the ferns and palms. In one corner is a grand piano.

The dining room, with a long mahogany table and large paintings, opens up onto a stone terrace above a sunken garage. The terrace is partially covered with a wooden trellis, overgrown in summer with plump juicy grapes.

Feliński Street, with No. 23 seen through trees at right

Feliński Street No. 23   *Garden of Feliński Street No. 23*

Off the entry hall to the right is a small efficiency apartment and to the left are the kitchen and the maids' quarters.

Upstairs the bedrooms are organized around a huge tiled bathroom with a big skylight. Since the room is so large, a painting easel has been set up for me under the skylight. My parents see in me a future watercolor artist. This arrangement is meant to encourage me in that direction.

Between the living room and dining room is my father's inner sanctum—the family library. In old, solid bookcases behind glass doors are the family's treasures—a large collection of books.

It is in this room that I explore the wonders of the world. Now that I am aware of becoming a man, the literature of Zola and Żeromski takes me into a forbidden world.

But the world of the battle of Grünwald, where Polish knights in tank armor with tall and heavy steel wings, mounted with feathers, destroy the Knights of the Black Cross—this is the one which gives me the greatest pleasure.

Reading the unending stories of the countless insurrections and fights and aggression against the Poles by the Germans, the Russians, the Turks, and the Tartars, I feel a special thrill. The characters in these books have become my friends.

My parents' and my sister's bedrooms open up onto a balcony running the length of the house. Climbing over the railing are espaliered trees, which in season bear soft, fuzzy peaches and juicy apricots. I have the run of the house. The attic and flat roof are where I kept my large white pigeon colony. I made them fly in formation over the whole suburb of Żoliborz. They would swing over Wilson Square and then, after measured formation flying, return to their home base. But then they started ruining my father's garden, and I was told to give up my pigeons.

So I have retreated to the basement where I have started to raise royal white domestic rabbits. They stamp their feet when they are hungry, and the noise can be heard in every corner of the house. The original pair multiplied overnight, and now there are so many that I cannot keep up with feeding them all, even with the help of the servants.

I use the floor of my bedroom to stage my wars. I have a whole unit of self-propelled tanks and fast-firing field guns. The tank treads tend to crush the soft lead pieces, so that I have to keep bringing in reinforcements by melting down the broken battalions and casting new ones. I am the general of the invading as well as of the defending forces. I hate to share my command and my battles with anyone!

Author—1934 (age five)

35

TUESDAY, JANUARY 2

Mother and I have been looking at maps today, picking out the location of our house in the northern part of Warsaw, in the suburb called Żoliborz, close to Wilson Square and not far from the Vistula. Studying the map reminds us that Żoliborz is a strategic spot for the Germans because it commands a view of the Vistula and the residential district of Praga, from which the main highways lead to the plains of the Ukraine and to Russia. Westward are the Powązki Cemetery, the boulevards leading out of the city to the villages and farmlands of central Poland, and the main roads to Germany. To the north are the sand dunes of Bielany and the vast stretch of wilderness of the Great Kampinoska Forest. The Warsaw–Gdańsk railway line, which connects the capital with the hinterlands and with the great ports of the Baltic Sea, is its boundary on the south.

WEDNESDAY, JANUARY 3

Mother is sick today. This is the opportunity I have been waiting for—I have her to myself all day. She has been reminiscing about the past. The war makes one do that, she says. She was born near Tarnów, in southeastern Poland, and her grandfather was a large landowner with many villages on his estate. She can trace her ancestors back to King Leszczyński and the palace at Baranowice. Mother described its elegant Renaissance courtyard, the beautiful garden, and its many other splendors, but to me it was exciting because it had served as a fortification against the Turkish and Tartar invasions. Mother is so different from Father. I love them both, of course, but each one in different ways.

THURSDAY, JANUARY 4

The effects of the invasion bombing last autumn are felt even now. Just today they found the remains of more bodies under the rubble, and people are still trying to get glass to mend their broken windows. The Germans stopped some Jews on the street this afternoon and arrested them for not wearing their Star of David armbands.

Baranowice Palace

TUESDAY, FEBRUARY 13

Today is Father's and my Name's Day, but he didn't get home from the office until late. Mother tried to arrange something special, and we waited anxiously for his arrival. After dinner, Father told me his life story.

Before the First World War, Father went to France to study. When the war broke out he returned to Poland and joined Piłsudski's Legions to fight the Russians. After the war he met and married Mother, worked with our diplomatic mission in Moscow, and then went back to France for political and economic studies at the Sorbonne.

In 1934 his friend and fellow legionnaire, Stefan Starzyński, was appointed City President of Warsaw, and a year later my father joined him as one of the vice-presidents. Then, in 1938, Father went to Germany to purchase buses for Warsaw's transportation system. There he had an opportunity to see the tremendous buildup of armaments. He says it was very clear then that war was coming.

FRIDAY, FEBRUARY 16

Aunt Stacha has been living with us since last October, after her house was destroyed by a German bomb. She is my father's sister, and, like him, a great patriot, cursing the Germans and the Russians in a single breath. As my room is next to hers, I don't miss much.

Aunt Stacha's room is filled with a large collection of antique furniture belonging to my Uncle Władek, her other brother, which he abandoned there when he and his bride escaped with the Polish Government, through Rumania to France, at the start of the war. Uncle Władek was one of our delegates to the League of Nations in Geneva. Aunt Stacha refuses to let a single piece be moved and spends her days polishing the furniture in preparation for her brother's return. She also guards a collection of fine paintings which Uncle Norbert had given her in better days. I like spending time with Aunt Stacha. She gives me tea and poppy seed cake and reminisces about her childhood and my grandmother, a well-known revolutionary of her generation.

TUESDAY, FEBRUARY 20

Today I went to the library to get a new supply of books, only to find that the Germans closed it last week. That makes me mad.

MONDAY, FEBRUARY 26

Uncle Norbert came to the house today; I had not seen him since Father's and my Name's Day. Everyone except Aunt Stacha loves to see him. She flees to her room as soon as he enters the front door. They are either estranged or divorced, but no one will talk to me about it, so I am not sure which.

Uncle Norbert is a big man. He looks a little unkempt with his baggy clothes and mussy hair, but he does have a great charm and warmth. His humor is keen and robust, his voice booming. I love him, not only because he makes me laugh, but also because he doesn't mind spending time talking to me and treating me as a grown-up, not a child.

SUNDAY, MARCH 3

My eleventh birthday.

In the evening Father invited me to his library to continue our discussion about the family. Father is a powerfully built man but gentle and patient most of the time. Sometimes, though, he flies off the handle at my mother, which frightens me. Yet now, in spite of the day's pressures, he looks at me in a kind way, his gray blue eyes friendly.

Like Mother, Father is fond of reminiscing about his family. His paternal grandfather was a doctor, and one of the leading citizens of Radomsk, a small town south of Warsaw, on the way to Cracow. He married the daughter of a well-known Polish patriot, became quite wealthy and had an elegant and large house in Radomsk.

He picked as a wife for his only son a well-known Polish writer, the daughter of a close friend. But the son (my grandfather) preferred to pick his own wife and married a salesgirl, the daughter of a Warsaw shoemaker. Angered at this challenge to his authority, my great-grandfather disinherited his son and cut off relations with his new family. Father saw him only once.

Father was particularly fond of his maternal grandfather, who would let the boy sit at his feet in the dingy, one-room shop where he made and repaired shoes. He would take a generous pinch of tobacco, fill his enormous nose, and sneeze lustily. My father listened day after day to his grandfather tell of his dreams of an independent Poland.

SUNDAY, MARCH 10

Uncle Norbert came for dinner tonight. After he left, Father talked to me about him. He says that Uncle Norbert was his tutor and mentor, which rather surprised me, for Uncle was a revolutionary in his youth and was arrested and interrogated several times by the Tsarist police. Later he belonged to the most active political opposition to Marshal Piłsudski and was arrested and imprisoned by the Polish police. He was also the Minister of the Interior and later Mayor of Łódż.

Father says Uncle Norbert is a dreamer, an idealist, a poet, and a philosopher. Time is running out on him, however, and he must accomplish his ideals soon. He is restless and driven with a single mission in life—to fight tyranny.

TUESDAY, MARCH 12

The house is now filled with relatives and friends, mostly women; they have all come as refugees, after being bombed, or forced, out of their homes. Aunt Wanda is the exception. She occupies the efficiency apartment on the first floor and moves about the house quietly and gracefully. She is a professional translator and has come back from Japan, where she worked in the diplomatic service. I like being invited to her room. She flutters about in her brightly colored kimonos, telling me mysterious stories and letting me touch her collection of treasures: blue and yellow wooden birds, intricately carved ivory globes enclosed one within the other, and strange-sounding Japanese musical instruments. Aunt Wanda is an excellent pianist, and I like her to play for me.

FRIDAY, MARCH 15

Today "Aunt" Hala moved into our upstairs apartment with her daughter. The Germans have thrown them out of Bydgoszcz. "Uncle" Julian, Father's friend and Governor of Bydgoszcz, escaped abroad. I went to talk to "Aunt" Hala about the summer I spent with them before the war. When I arrived at the Governor's mansion, "Aunt" Hala was entertaining officers from the armored battalion holding maneuvers in the nearby woods. Some of them helped "Aunt" Hala to teach me how to swim in the river. Others danced with her at the officers' mess. I kept begging them to let me ride in the tanks, and finally Major Rawkowski took me with him in his observation tank during maneuvers. I wish Father could have seen me!

When we got back to Bydgoszcz that evening we went to see the movie *The Great Dictator* with Charlie Chaplin. He was better than all the clowns in the Warsaw circus. I couldn't understand why the large German population of Bydgoszcz disapproved of the film.

MONDAY, MARCH 25

It is Easter, and Zula and I spent today visiting churches. The symbolic grave inside Saint Anne's Church was drawing a crowd. The line was blocks' long and we had to start at the foot of the Mickiewicz monument. It took two and a half hours before we were inside and in front of the grave, but the wait was worth it. The scene was unmistakenly tied to the siege of Warsaw, dramatically lit and well designed. Among the ruins of the city rested the body of Christ, decorated with red and white flowers. The Cross of burnt timber could be seen through a blackened window—a reminder of last September—in the suffering city of crosses and graves. It is an obvious patriotic manifestation and everyone—almost everyone—understands its meaning. Except the two German soldiers in front of us who saw the drama in the religious context alone, whispering to each other, "Very beautiful."

SATURDAY, MARCH 30

Mother tells me that the parish priest from Saint Anne's Church has been arrested by the Gestapo and taken to Pawiak Prison. I wonder what the Germans want with a priest?

MONDAY, APRIL 1

The monthly rations have been cut, and we have to make the coupons go even farther now. For each person, per month, we are allowed only two hundred and fifty grams of bread; two hundred and fifty grams each of meat and of sugar; two eggs; and one small box of matches. So, we have to buy food on the Black Market. I went with Mother today to Kerceli Square. Here one can get not only food but also everything else—clothes, furniture, china and jewelry. People are selling their possessions in order to get money to live, but prices are very, very high.

Mother says many people are without work, and even those with jobs find their salaries are not sufficient to live on. So, they have to find other ways to survive. The German clerks and soldiers can be tempted by money, and they buy and sell many things. Mother sold some silver, and we bought food. Then we went to see my mother's sister, Aunt Zosia, who lives in Praga. She is a nurse and works in a Polish hospital there. The Germans have their own hospitals.

MONDAY, APRIL 8

Today I went to the Hotel Bristol, near Piłsudski Square, just because it is off limits to us, and I don't like being told where I can or cannot go in my own city. The hotel has been turned into a billet for German officers, and the dining room and lobby are marked NUR FÜR DEUTSCHE (For Germans Only). It is a dangerous place for me to go, but I like the excitement of it. The dining room was crowded. I sat at a corner table and hid myself behind the *Warschauer Zeitung* which I had bought in the lobby. I tried to affect German arrogance and, since I am extremely tall and well developed for my age, I managed with my knowledge of German and the right clothes to pass for one of them. I was fascinated by the "supermen" in their handsome uniforms, and incredulously watched them consume huge tankards of beer and quantities of sauerkraut.

There were also tall, blonde women to be seen with German soldiers or officers both at the hotel and on the nearby streets. They were German women. Very few Poles come to this area, and Polish girls hardly ever fraternize with German soldiers.

But there are exceptions. Danusia is one. She and I went to school together, a grade school near the Zoological Gardens across the Vistula in Praga. I had often played in the gardens there, and at times the Zoo Director would let me play with some of the animals. Sometimes Danusia would come with me.

I had lost track of Danusia after I left the Praga school and did not see her again until today, when I chanced upon her at the Hotel Bristol. Walking in front of the hotel, I couldn't believe my eyes when I saw her strolling along the street on the arm of a German soldier. They disappeared into the Saski Gardens. I am disgusted to think that Danusia can turn traitor like this.

WEDNESDAY, APRIL 17

From the *Warschauer Zeitung* at the Hotel Bristol I glean various bits of information. Today the paper carried an interview with the German health director of the Warsaw region, in which he said that the Jewish district of Warsaw should be separated from the rest of the city because the Jews are carriers of typhus. The near future, he predicted, will show the form this separation will take. This is incredible—do the Germans actually believe their own propaganda? They surely don't expect the Poles to swallow it!

SUNDAY, APRIL 21

Before the war Mother had maids, and we had a governess, so she had plenty of free time for welfare work. Father also attended many social events, and they often went to the theater and opera. Now, however, Poles have stopped going to the theater or concerts, although some give concerts at home. Mostly, they play music by Chopin, which is banned by the Germans.

Mother's life has changed completely. It is a full-time job just trying to feed the family and the others who have come to live in our house. She has started going three or four times a week to a small village called Baniocha, bringing back fruit and vegetables to sell.

FRIDAY, MAY 3

Our National Holiday—to mark the occasion, the Germans rounded people up on the squares of Żoliborz yesterday. They were taken away in military trucks, and nobody seems to know where or why. Is this the Germans' new way of getting people for their labor camps? On the way to see Zula today I noticed that somebody has put red and white flowers on the Tomb of the Unknown Soldier on Piłsudski Square, and that the flame on the tomb is still burning.

SATURDAY, MAY 4

Some of my friends and I began our own private war against the Germans today. I went to the street corners around Żoliborz and with a struggle tore down five or six wooden signboards, and carried them home on my bicycle. It wasn't easy, and I also had to watch out for patrols or military and police cars. The signs I got today were:

K.W.: KOMMANDO DER WEHRMACHT
K.L.: KOMMANDO DER LUFTWAFFE
SS.K.: KOMMANDO DER SCHUTZSTAFFELN
A.O.K.: ARMEEOBERKOMMANDO
H.G.: HEERESGRUPPE

SUNDAY, MAY 5

Today I went back to one of the street corners where I took down the signs yesterday. The German driver of a big military truck stopped and asked for directions, and I made sure he was sent completely the wrong way. A lot of trucks and cars could be seen wandering around the streets later, losing precious time and gasoline and cursing the Poles. However, the street signs were put back up this afternoon, so we will have to repeat our performance tonight after curfew.

The anchor sign of Fighting Poland (PW: Polska Walcząca)

45

SUNDAY, MAY 12

Everywhere you go there are new indications of resistance: on buildings and signboards you can see the anchor sign POLSKA WALCZĄCA (Fighting Poland). Others are POLSKA ZWYCIĘŻY (Poland Will Win); DEUTSCHLAND KAPUT; or the sign of the turtle, which is the symbol of a work slowdown. A large wooden German victory sign, inscribed DEUTSCHLAND SIEGT AN ALLEN FRONTEN (Germany Wins on All Fronts), was burned tonight. It has given me an idea.

MONDAY, MAY 13

Another big manhunt was mounted today on Wilson Square, between our house and Czarniecki Street. The Germans stopped all streetcars and, again, took people away in enclosed army trucks.

TUESDAY, MAY 14

At five o'clock this evening, near the corner of Feliński Street and Wilson Square, a friend and I came into the square, wheeling our bicycles. We propped them against a building, and I went over to some old women still selling bread under the wooden signboard. After they heard what I had to say, the old women vanished. Quickly taking a bottle filled with liquid out of his pocket, my friend threw it as hard as he could against the signboard. The bottle broke into pieces and the liquid soaked into the posters. Then, he quickly struck a match and the whole of Wilson Square was lit up.

At the same second, three Germans walked around the corner on the other side of the square. As soon as we saw them, my friend and I jumped onto our bicycles and pedaled away as fast as we could. Fortunately for us, the Germans were on foot and couldn't catch up with us.

WEDNESDAY, MAY 15

On a trip to the city today, I noticed that the rubble around Bonifraterska Street is being used to build a huge wall. I wonder what's going on?

The Wall going up, Summer 1940

THURSDAY, MAY 16

The wooden billboard near Meinl's store on Wilson Square has already been replaced and, again, official posters are put up every day by the Germans. These posters call on the Polish people to stop killing the Germans, or they carry Fischer's orders about forced labor, Krüger's police regulations pertaining to Jews, or posters of German propaganda. These posters no sooner go up than they are defaced, and today many were pasted over with posters and announcements of our own. Good for us!

SATURDAY, MAY 18

My father appealed to the population today to be careful of the dud shells which are strewn on the streets and parks. I wonder what he would say if he knew what I am doing these days, and especially that I am planning to get a pistol.

MONDAY, MAY 20

Today Father came home from work in a very agitated state. The Germans tried to organize a pogrom in the area around Długa Street. They gathered up a bunch of criminal prisoners and used them as anti-Semitic agitators. Father says that although *this* attempt to direct violence against Jews and their property failed because the majority of Poles by far flatly refused to have anything to do with it, steps must be taken to ensure that future attempts also fail.

Father says he has contacted the Underground and asked them to locate any collaborators involved with a view to punishing them severely. He is also sending a letter to the German city authorities, demanding an immediate end to such organized criminal activities.

As I listened to my father, I remembered reading of the famous *Kristallnacht* in Germany several years ago, and hoped that the Germans weren't trying to create a repetition of that event here. In any case, I am puzzled, because the Germans have lumped all Poles together (Christians and Jews alike), describing our nation as one of "subhumans" like the gypsies.

Statue of Chopin (postwar replica)

48

TUESDAY, MAY 28

Frank and Fischer today staged a parade of new detachments of German police troops. On the way to Zula's I saw Frank himself in an open touring car, standing and staring at the statue of Chopin in Łazienki Park.

FRIDAY, MAY 31

Father tells me the Germans have removed the statue of Chopin and are going to melt it down. Another attack on our pride!

FRIDAY, JUNE 7

We heard today that France has fallen. The courtyard at Brühl Palace, Fischer's headquarters, was covered in banners with the twisted cross, and full of Germans shouting, "*Sieg Heil!*" How I hate that cry.

MONDAY, JUNE 10

This afternoon I saw Ludwig Leist's latest proclamation, forbidding private lessons. That won't stop us! But I guess we'll have to take more care than ever to keep school secret.

FRIDAY, JUNE 28

What a bang! The Germans dynamited the Citadel fortifications near Żoliborz today. I saw it from Wilson Square.

Leist has ordered that all signs must be bilingual—German and Polish, or German and Hebrew. "Divide and conquer," as Mrs. Bernardyńska says.

MONDAY, JULY 1

This morning's newspaper carried a notice that only Jews are to be allowed to move into the area where the wall around Bonifraterska Street is being constructed. I wish I could discover what this really means.

WEDNESDAY, JULY 3

At seven o'clock this morning my father was in the bathroom, and Mother was in the bedroom doing her hair, when I heard a noise on the front steps. Then four German policemen entered and went up to my parents' bedroom on the second floor. Saying nothing, they opened the linen closet and threw everything out on the floor. Among the linens they found a copy of *Life* magazine. They immediately took Father to the Gestapo. How long this time? I am actually as scared and upset as my mother is, but I am trying hard to be brave and to help her.

THURSDAY, JULY 4

A well-known Polish lady, who had hidden some of Uncle Norbert's art collection for him, to keep it from being confiscated by the Germans, came to the house today. She was very nervous and told us that Uncle was arrested yesterday at her apartment by the Gestapo and taken to Pawiak Prison. Aunt Stacha's alienation from Uncle Norbert is total, but it did not stop her from what she did now. She took two of his paintings out of their heavy gilt frames, made a flat package out of them, and left the house.

The Germans are not supposed to be subject to bribes, but everyone knows about their art collections. Many people give up their best possessions in this way.

Aunt Stacha was on her way to a "confidence" man to ask him to use the paintings to free Uncle Norbert. When she came home she seemed downcast, as if her mission had failed.

MONDAY, JULY 8

Father is back from prison, pale and solemn and very quiet. He saw Uncle Norbert there, but they will not release him. I am really beginning to fear for my father's life, not to mention worrying about the rest of the family.

FRIDAY, JULY 12

My parents have decided to mortgage our house at Feliński Street in order to raise enough money to keep us alive. While the arrangements are being made, we are going to the countryside for a month.

MONDAY, JULY 15

Father took us today to Radzymin near Warsaw. We are staying in an old house in a big park with many trees. Father will have to return to Warsaw immediately, of course, and I hate to see him go.

SATURDAY, JULY 20

This place reminds me of Uncle Juzek's place near Równe in eastern Poland, where Mother took me a few summers ago. I keep asking what has happened to him, and she says sadly that she does not know.

I remember the old Ukrainian peasant who spat into the haystack. Old Mikuś spat all the time; he spat on the ground when loading the haywagon that we were sitting on; he spat when holding the reins; and he spat when unloading the bales. Old Mikuś never talked, and his bristly unshaven face fascinated me. He smelled like sour cabbage.

He would never give me a ride unless I first gave him a hand-rolled *machorka* cigarette. Staś Bimber, the stableboy, told me that this was the unspoken law of Old Mikuś—no *machorka*, no ride. One day, on the way from Równe in a bouncing carriage pulled by two frisky white horses, my mother told me that Uncle Juzek had acquired the farm after the First World War. He was a good officer, and Piłsudski gave him this large farm in the Ukraine as a reward for his bravery in fighting the Russians.

As we rumbled over the dust-covered roads, I wondered why my father, who had also fought the Russians, had not been given a farm.

When we had arrived at the farm, Uncle and his family were

51

waiting for us under the shade of the large portico of the white-painted house.

Kasztan was my horse—a young gelding whose coat was the color of the shining chestnuts I used to pick in the Zoological Gardens in Warsaw. Uncle's old Warrant Officer, Pan Paweł, would bring Kasztan to the front porch and help me onto his bare back. I rode along dusty country roads, stopping frequently under the large trees to pick the juicy red and white cherries.

I remember one particularly hot, endless day, when I made at least twelve trips between the fields and the farm on the ten-foot-high haywagon. As it swayed from side to side, seemingly ready to overturn at any minute, I counted the *machorka* cigarettes I gave Old Mikuś. Looking down at him on the seat below me, his head enshrouded in billowing clouds of black smoke from the native tobacco, I made up my mind: the next cigarette I rolled would be for me! Licking the thin white paper with my tongue, the way Old Mikuś had shown me, I made several attempts at lighting the cigarette and took my first puff. The smoke seemed to fill my entire body, and my head throbbed. The smoke curled into my eyes, and they streamed with tears. I felt as bad as the time that Kasztan kicked me in the stomach when I approached him without warning from behind.

I became aware of Staś staring at me with his cowlike eyes, in mocking silence. I remembered that when we had a fist fight the previous week, he had run into his hut and had then come after me with a big, sharp axe. I had run like hell, to get home and away from the crazy Ukrainian bastard! Now, he sat there smiling like a big toad. Stubbornly, I smoked all the way home. When we reached the hayloft, I slid off the wagon without any trouble, but then my legs gave out, and I curled up in agony on the ground. I was dying! Needless to say, I got no sympathy from anyone.

THURSDAY, AUGUST 15

We came back to Warsaw today, and it was so good to see Father again. I went out later to Wilson Square and bought a copy of a new paper, *The Jewish Gazette*, published by the Germans in Cracow. It seems as anti-Catholic as the other German newspaper, the

New Warsaw Courier, is anti-Semitic. Again, I wondered if the Germans could really believe their own propaganda, and, again, Father told me, "Never underestimate the Germans."

SUNDAY, SEPTEMBER 1

The final insult—to celebrate the first anniversary of the invasion of Poland, Fischer today renamed Piłsudski Square as Adolf Hitler Platz in a ceremony with band and flags. A great wooden frame now covers the statue of Prince Poniatowski. No patriotic Pole attended the ceremony, of course, but the newspapers were full of it.

Piłsudski Square about to be renamed Adolf Hitler Platz, marking first anniversary of the German invasion

THURSDAY, SEPTEMBER 19

Another big manhunt on Wilson Square and Mickiewicz Street took place today, but we have no idea of how many people were rounded up and taken away. It's getting scary.

MONDAY, SEPTEMBER 30

I noticed a new sign on the streetcars today—some are now marked *Tylko dla Żydów* (For Jews Only). What will they do next!

53

A roundup, 1940

An execution, 1940

54

The New Order

SATURDAY, OCTOBER 5

Frank is in Warsaw to celebrate the anniversary of Hitler's victory parade. The city is covered in flags, and full of SS and police troops. I tried to go to Zula's, but the streets were roped off so I had to turn back. I am getting more and more restless at having my freedom of movement restricted.

SATURDAY, OCTOBER 12

I was passing through Wilson Square today, as the public address speaker above the main entrance to Żeromski Park suddenly blared across the square. Everyone came to a halt, as the words of Fischer filled the air. The voice announced the division of the city into three separate and distinct housing areas: German, Polish, and Jewish. Families which the Germans consider to belong to one group, but who now live in one of the other areas, are given only until the end of the month to move from their homes and find new ones. People are shocked and frightened. I wonder what will happen to Zula and her mother; they still have no news of Zula's father, an army officer who was taken prisoner in September 1939.

SUNDAY, OCTOBER 13

I walked to a nearby café this morning and called Zula. She has heard yesterday's news, too, and she is as depressed and worried as I am.

Tonight I heard my father telling my mother that Adam Czerniaków, head of the Jewish Council, has been told officially of the creation by the Germans of the Warsaw Ghetto, and that Czerniaków has been instructed to form a thousand-man Jewish police force for service within the Ghetto walls. I wanted to ask Father about it, but I knew he'd be angry that I'd been eavesdropping.

MONDAY, OCTOBER 14

There is now frantic activity throughout the city, with Christian and Jewish families alike packing their refugee allowances of twenty-five kilograms per person and trying to get moved to their new districts before the end of the month. The remainder of their goods has to be left behind—all furniture and other things which belong to Christian Poles who are moving out of the newly created Ghetto, and those belonging to Jewish Poles moving into the Ghetto from other parts of Warsaw.

Some people are moving their precious possessions in hand-carts or horse-drawn wagons; others are going on foot, carrying

The move to the Ghetto, 1940

57

their belongings in sheets and sacks slung over their shoulders. The Germans are making coolies out of the Poles—we even have rickshaws on the streets now.

MONDAY, OCTOBER 28

I roamed around the city today, on foot and by streetcar. The *New Warsaw Courier* now carries the names of the streets which form the boundaries of the Jewish "residential" district. I had bought the paper this morning and decided to spend the day inspecting the area for myself. I got off the Żoliborz streetcar at Bonifraterska Street and Muranów Square, and crossed the area I know so well—through Nalewki and Gęsia Streets, past Krasiński Park, and across Tłomackie Square with its large synagogue. The residential streets are composed mainly of three- to five-story buildings with elegant facades of stone and wrought-iron balconies. When I had been here before I was fascinated by the bagel sellers, the aroma of cooking, and the black-garbed men with flowing beards huddled together and talking with warm, enthusiastic words. This time, life on the sidewalks is different—people are rushing about, nervously jostling each other. Even old people are pushing carts. On Chłodna, Gęsia, and Nalewki Streets, and many others as well, the streetcar tracks have been torn up where the red brick wall has been constructed.

When I reached the Iron Gate Square, I continued on, and then came to Mirowski Square, flanked by the enormous market hall buildings. I suddenly realized that the newspaper I had read at home had described this area as the "finger" which would split the Ghetto into two parts. What is now to be the first and largest part of the Ghetto already contains predominantly Jewish, lower-middle-class and working-class families.

In front of me, the wall ran all the way to the Jewish section of Powązki Cemetery, then turned along Stawki Street and Muranów Square, which I had entered a couple of hours ago.

This area was to the northwest of me, as I stood on Mirowski Square. Behind me and to the left was the smaller Ghetto, its boundary starting at the corner of Chłodna Street; running southwest along Żelazna Street; turning and running along the elegant

Interior of Tłomackie Synagogue

and affluent Sienna Street; up Wielka Street; back to the Iron Gate Square; and on to Mirowski Square again.

Standing on Mirowski Square, I wondered where Zula and her family would be moving to. I have had no contact with her since my last phone call, because her mother said I should stay away until they find a new home and get moved.

As I turned back to catch the streetcar home, I walked outside the wall on Żelazna, Wolności, and Okopowa Streets. When I returned from my "inspection," I was dead tired—I must have walked more than fifteen kilometers. Looking at the map really depressed and scared me, as it brought home to me just how large an area of the city was being enclosed.

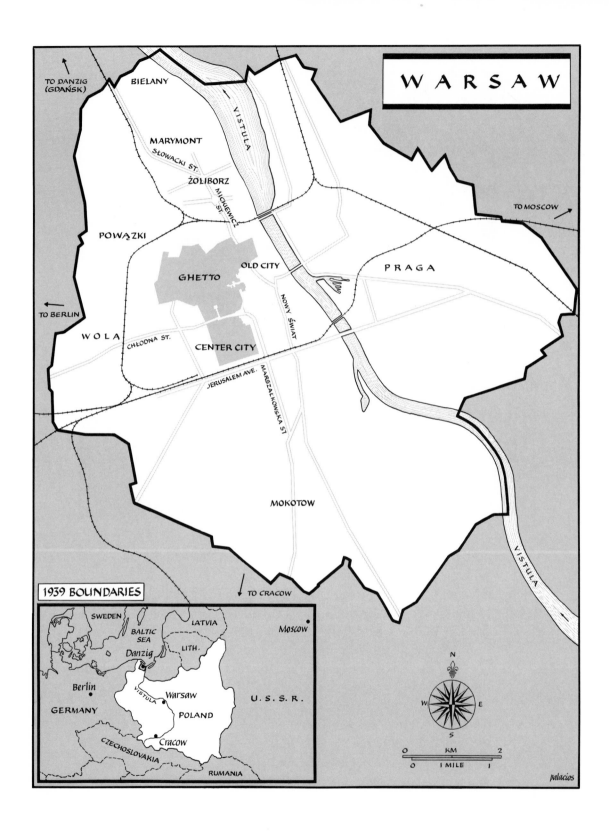

WARSAW

TO DANZIG
(GDAŃSK)

BIELANY

VISTULA

MARYMONT

SŁOWACKI ST.

ŻOLIBORZ

MICKIEWICZ ST.

TO MOSCOW

POWĄZKI

GHETTO

OLD CITY

PRAGA

NOWY ŚWIAT

TO BERLIN

WOLA

CHŁODNA ST.

CENTER CITY

JERUSALEM AVE.

MARSZAŁKOWSKA ST

MOKOTOW

TO CRACOW

VISTULA

1939 BOUNDARIES

SWEDEN

LATVIA

BALTIC
SEA

LITH.

Moscow

Danzig

Berlin

VISTULA

Warsaw

GERMANY

POLAND

U.S.S.R.

Cracow

CZECHOSLOVAKIA

RUMANIA

N

W

E

S

0   KM   2

0   1 MILE   1

palacios

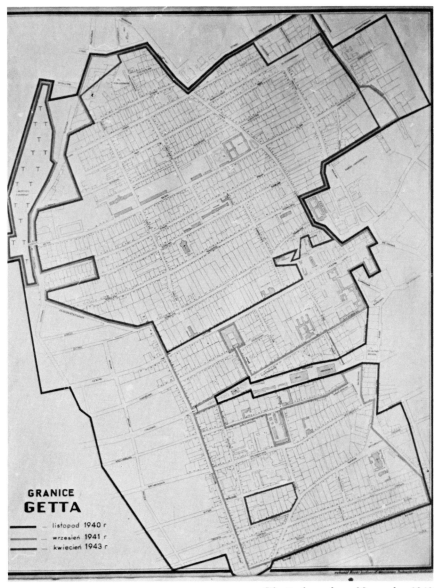

GRANICE
GETTA

listopad 1940 r
wrzesień 1941 r
kwiecień 1943 r

Ghetto boundary, November 1940

FRIDAY, NOVEMBER 15

I went out on my rounds of the city again today. The "Red Wall" enclosing the Ghetto is now completed. I have called the wall that because of the color of the bricks from which it has been built. People are saying that the ten gates are heavily guarded, and nobody can come or leave without being questioned and searched at gunpoint. I find this hard to believe, but I can see for myself that the guards at the gates do have specially trained attack dogs on short leashes. Traffic through these gates is now also infrequent, but I am puzzled because the city streetcars are still running through the Ghetto on the old tracks.

WEDNESDAY, NOVEMBER 20

I have decided to find out more about what the enclosing of the Ghetto means. So, I took the streetcar today and discovered that, although the cars do still run through the Ghetto, they enter at one gate and pass through the crowded streets at full speed without stopping. Without discharging or picking up passengers, they then leave by the gate at the other end. On the step of the platform of each car is a member of the Polish "Blue" Police, with both hands tightly gripping the vertical railings. These police are usually referred to as "Blues" because of the color of their uniforms, and I am told it is their responsibility to see that nobody jumps on or off the moving vehicles.

SATURDAY, NOVEMBER 30

Ratajski, the Prime Minister's plenipotentiary, came to see my father today. Father told him of the terrible conditions inside and outside the Ghetto and said he wondered whether he should continue in office under these circumstances.

Ratajski said that the activities of the Polish City Administration are absolutely necessary and will give Father great opportunities to instigate sabotage and to help the Underground. It would be very good if Father could retain the entire staff and organization of City Hall until liberation. Ratajski feels that my father can perform a great service to the Underground, and to the citizens. He told Father that he must remain in his post and that, in fact, he will not be allowed to leave it except under special circumstances.

Ratajski's instructions were clear—this was an order.

THURSDAY, DECEMBER 12

It was a bitterly cold day today, which is Zula's birthday. She called me to say that her family had finished moving and gave me the address of the new place, so I went to see her.

Sitting in the last seat of the streetcar, I waited until we got close to Muranów Square. Just as the streetcar slowed to turn the corner into the square, the "Blue" policeman moved from the platform into the compartment to warm his hands. As he was lighting a cigarette, I quickly got up, jumped off the metal step, and mixed with the crowd; then I made my way to the address Zula had given me.

I could never in my life have imagined such crowded streets. Not only the sidewalks, but the roads as well were a hive of pushing, shoving humanity. Among the crowds were carts full of bedding and furniture, pulled or pushed by men and women, as they moved about from street to street in search of a home. Nalewki Street, one of the main streets, was bedlam, with people shouting and slipping on the icy surface. I found Zula and her mother finishing their midday meal in the single room which is now their bedroom, dining room, and living area. They share the kitchen and bathroom of this third-floor apartment with the owner, the widow of a cavalry officer. She has a room to herself, and the brother of the deceased, a lawyer who works with Czerniaków's Jewish Council, shares a third room with his two nephews.

Both Zula and her mother seemed pleased I had come and asked me to sit down and have some tea and bread. Zula hardly talked but just looked at me with sad, dark eyes. Her mother tried to be optimistic and said how really lucky they were to have friends who could take them in. She pointed to the three large French windows and the not unpleasant furniture in the room, and said how really luxurious it was for the times.

There was a knock on the door and the man of the house entered, a fellow about thirty; he gave me a strong, warm handshake after Zula's mother introduced me. After a hearty welcome, he said he had heard a great deal about me from Zula and was happy to have me with them. He then sat down and joined us in the frugal but tasty meal.

He told us there are now more than a quarter of a million people in this part of the city, but only 140,000 rooms. He spoke of the Germans having the audacity to create this great debacle in the name of health protection, by claiming that this area is typhoid-prone; 113,000 people (mostly Christians) have had to leave their homes here and another 138,000 (mostly Jews) have been forced to move behind the Wall. To make things worse, he went on, the Germans were now making every effort to separate Jews from the city not only by the Wall—they were also taking away their rights as Polish citizens and preventing them from maintaining contact with the city and national authorities. If this is true, no wonder my father is more and more despondent every time Czerniaków sees him at City Hall. I must ask him about it when I can.

Zula's mother shook her head, saying that they would not be able to accomplish this. The young man disagreed, and went on to say that Czerniaków had already complained in vain to the housing authorities about the present starvation-level diet, combined with the overcrowding, grossly inadequate sanitation facilities, and lack of fuel, all of which are creating conditions in which epidemics may indeed become reality. Zula's mother always gets straight to the point and she did so now, "If anybody can handle the situation, it is Adam Czerniaków. He is not afraid of anybody—including the Germans. I understand they call him 'that fresh Jew' because he is not taking any nonsense from them."

"True, true," the man broke in, "but how many Czerniaków's do we have here?"

It was getting dark in the room as the curfew hour approached, so I excused myself and, after an affectionate good-bye to Zula, jumped on the last streetcar leaving through the Bonifraterska Street Gate, fortunately almost empty and somehow without a police guard. That night I found it impossible to sleep, my mind churning away about what I had seen and heard today, and what it might mean.

WEDNESDAY, DECEMBER 18

A twelve-year-old classmate of mine, Jędrek, asked me to come to his house today, and to distract myself from the thought of what is happening to Zula, I went. He is a wizard at chemistry, who has learned enough to put his knowledge to practical use. He tells me he is building a small arsenal, and has asked me to help. I agreed eagerly, for I felt that finally I was getting a chance to do something constructive.

Jędrek lives on Krasiński Street, which is far enough away from home that my family will not get wind of my activities.

FRIDAY, DECEMBER 20

It is strictly against the law to have any weapons or explosives—the punishment could even be death—so Jędrek and I have to be very careful. We decided to look for dud artillery shells in the parks around Żoliborz today, and found three—two small ones and one large one; the last one was found not far from his house, in the grass median strip on Krasiński Street.

SATURDAY, DECEMBER 21

Last night, between the two of us, we were able to carry the two smaller shells to Jędrek's garage. But we had a problem with the third one. We finally managed to get a cart and rolled it to its destination. Today we tinkered with the shells until we got them open. Then we took out the gunpowder, which we put in jam jars and stored away carefully.

SUNDAY, DECEMBER 22

Jędrek says he now has what we really need: something with the greatest explosive power—nitroglycerin. So today we worked from early morning until late afternoon in his garage. The nitro was finally ready to be stored in test tubes. I had to get home before curfew, and Jędrek said he would wait for my return before carrying on. He promised he would just lock up and then go to his room right away. On the way home I realized that in the excitement I'd forgotten to ask Jędrek where on earth he had got the nitro in the first place; I'll have to ask him about it tomorrow.

MONDAY, DECEMBER 23

It snowed heavily last night, and this morning was fiercely cold and clear. I had planned to leave at noon to go to the garage, but in midmorning a neighbor came with a message. Mother broke the news that a terrible explosion had occurred. I grabbed my jacket and ran as fast as I could until I reached our "laboratory." The garage was a complete shambles.

My friend had already been taken to the hospital. I did not know until I got there what to expect, and I was horrified when I saw him. His right arm had been blown off.

TUESDAY, DECEMBER 24

Zula's situation and my friend's accident have put me in a dark mood for Christmas, and I am taking little part in the family activities. Mother wants to cheer us up and she has scrounged and saved for weeks to have the traditional *Wigilia*. I notice she is no longer wearing her beautiful diamond ring—she won't admit it, but I'm sure she has sold it to get money for food.

The tree is more beautiful than ever; the candles reflect the glistening ornaments; gifts are exchanged, and so are greetings and embraces; the wafer is broken to share the spirit of Christ; and the table is decorated with fruits, nuts, and flowers. Mother has even made something special out of the beet marmalade we have been eating lately. But something is lacking.

The traditional empty chair this year is for Uncle Norbert, from whom we have not heard since last summer when the gates of Pawiak Prison closed behind him. I cannot shake my melancholy mood, so I have left them all—Father, Mother, my aunts, my sister, the "guests" who now make their home with us, the maids, and our little dachshund, Szkut—and have come to the quiet of my room to be alone.

66

1941

TUESDAY, JANUARY 7

This is a very sad day for us. Father has found out that early yester-day morning, in the bitter cold and heavy snow, five hundred pris-oners were moved from Pawiak Prison to the Warsaw West Station. Among them was Uncle Norbert, and also many other leading po-litical figures. They were loaded onto unheated cattle trains which moved out of the city going south toward Cracow—probably on the way to a concentration camp. My anger is increasing—the Ger-mans have taken my favorite Uncle away. I would like to shout, to scream, and, above all, to fight. But it seems all we can do now is wait, and try to control our fears.

An arrest, 1941

SUNDAY, JANUARY 12

I woke up to the screaming of sirens in the night, that banshee wail that turns your blood cold. The Gestapo seemed to be all over Żoli-borz, and probably many people were arrested. After I fell asleep again, I had a nightmare in which Uncle Norbert appeared and stood by my bed. He looked haggard, sick, and lonely. His eyes seemed to plead: Come and help me; get me out of this place, Julek. Get me out!

69

MONDAY, JANUARY 20

Mother told me today that she has received news about Uncle Norbert. He has been taken to the concentration camp which the Germans have built at Oświęcim near Cracow—Auschwitz. Mother is terribly upset, but I try to console her with the fact that Uncle Norbert is at least still alive. Still, it is a terrible shock to me. All I hear of such places is of people starving to death, poisonous gases, execution squads, and hangings. Horror follows upon horror, and always there is fear—fear of the truth and fear of the unknown even more.

SATURDAY, JANUARY 25

Mother introduced me today to the real estate lady who sold us our house in the country at Baniocha. Mrs. Zofia Filipkiewicz is a close friend of my grandmother's, and Mother says it was kind of her to find such a nice place for us.

I kissed Mrs. Filipkiewicz's hand and unlike that of other old ladies, her skin was soft and smooth, and I actually touched it with my lips; usually I hate kissing old ladies' hands, all blotchy and wrinkled, and had learned long ago to slide my thumb up as I took their hand so that I kissed my own skin rather than theirs!

Mrs. Filipkiewicz was different, and she said that she hoped I would have lots of good times at Baniocha, especially when the war was over. A nice lady!

FRIDAY, JANUARY 31

Father told us today that another trainload of Pawiak prisoners has been taken to Auschwitz.

Every day I become more outraged—how can the Germans get away with it? How can grown men be herded together and taken off in trains like cattle? Why don't they fight, or at least try to run away? I think I would rather die fighting than be treated like this. But when I say this to my father, he tells me that there's more to it than that, and that I shouldn't make such critical statements on things I don't understand.

MONDAY, FEBRUARY 3

This morning I saw a big van moving slowly in front of our house. On top of the van was a silently revolving antenna, and I ran down to Aunt Stacha's room to ask her about it. She said the Germans were probably searching for secret radio equipment, particularly transmitters. The search continued all day with hundreds of German police checking house by house in Lower Żoliborz. They missed us. So after all, someone *is* trying to tell the world what is going on here! But, why don't the Allies come and bomb the railroad lines, bomb Berlin, or do *something* to stop this terrorization, humiliation, and killing of the Poles—Christians and Jews alike?

MONDAY, FEBRUARY 24

Staszek, the young man who lives in our basement and takes care of the furnace, went to the store this morning as usual to buy milk and bread, but he did not come back. I went out to look for him, and a neighbor said she thought he was among the people the Germans rounded up on Wilson Square and took away. She said because he is young, strong, and healthy, it probably means he is on his way to a forced-labor camp in Germany. I went to see his father, a violinmaker who uses our basement workshop. He was varnishing his latest instrument, and when he heard the news of his son's arrest, he just sat down on the bench, held his head in his hands, and cried silently. I didn't know how to comfort him, so I said nothing; but I wanted to tell the old man that I, too, was grieving and would miss Staszek. He had been my friend, and he had never treated me as a child, although he was already a young man.

SATURDAY, MARCH 1

On the way home from classes today I got off the streetcar at Inwalidów Square and wandered around there. A new appeal has been posted, calling on all Poles with military training to volunteer for police units to guard Jewish forced-labor workshops and barracks. How outrageous, but also how stupid—they will get no such volunteers here!

MONDAY, MARCH 3

Today I celebrated my twelfth birthday and had the usual session with my father in his library. He has very little spare time now, but he did spend this evening with me.

Stefan Żeromski is one of my father's favorite authors, and Father read to me from Żeromski's *Reflections of a Field-Marshal:*

> There exists here in Poland a built-in, everlasting loyalty to the lost cause, unknown anywhere else in the world, brought out by the righteous heart, which can be seen only in a great act, in untainted honor, . . .

Then he read from a contemporary Polish writer, Adam Próchnik:

> The measure of courage must depend on the degree that it was an act of conscious will. History must distinguish accidental acts of bravery from those which are the expression of the interior needs of man.

Mother then joined us, and my father began recalling his friendship with President Starzyński. Starzyński had had ample opportunities, he said, to join the Polish Government-in-Exile during the Siege of Warsaw. On September 27, 1939, when the firing stopped, Marshal Śmigły-Rydz sent a plane from Rumania to Warsaw to pick up General Rómmel (the Commander-in-Chief of the Polish Armies) and Starzyński, to take them out of the city. They refused to be treated differently from the rest of the army and the civilian population, although Starzyński, above all, knew full well that Hitler would not forgive him for the public radio announcements which told the whole world how the Germans were bombing the hospitals and killing civilians.

Later, when I said goodnight to my mother, she said Father hadn't told the whole story. Evidently Starzyński had asked Father to go in his place, but he had refused. I am beginning to understand my father better, and I'm becoming more and more proud of him. Before the war I was often taunted in school for being a "bourgeois," and I suppose I had subconsciously blamed Father for my being the target of these insults. Now that I've grown up more, I realize how lucky and glad I am to be his son.

THURSDAY, MARCH 6

Today's *Information Bulletin* carries the Underground announcement that any participation of Poles in anti-Jewish actions is traitorous and will be punishable by death, the sentence being passed by the Underground Court. I keep asking what the Jews have done to the Germans that they are receiving treatment worse than that handed out to other Poles. I know they are different, because they wear different clothes and don't speak our language, but, as Father now reminds me, that is only if they are Orthodox Jews—there are even more who dress and speak as we do, and who live in the same neighborhoods of Warsaw. But to be anti-Semitic *now* means you are not only turning against people from your own country—it means you are helping the Germans, and that I can't comprehend.

SATURDAY, MARCH 15

Today I heard shots on Polish Army Avenue and ran out onto the terrace to see what was happening. The shots came nearer and a young man ran into the driveway and called to me to hide him. I

Streetcar under footbridge connecting the Little Ghetto to the Big Ghetto

The Wall

A search at a Ghetto gate

74

pulled him up onto the terrace and took him into the dining room, just in time before some policemen ran by. I took him to the attic where I used to keep my pigeons. He calmed down, and after a while he asked me to check if all was clear before he left.

MONDAY, MARCH 17

Czerniaków saw my father in his office today and told him he had got a letter from Fischer appointing him "Mayor" of the Ghetto. Father says it is one more step toward isolation of the Ghetto by the Germans.

WEDNESDAY, MARCH 19

I went to the city today. All gates to the Ghetto are now closed and the streetcars have been rerouted outside the Wall. The Germans obviously do mean to isolate the Ghetto from the rest of the city! But why?

A Ghetto gate

THURSDAY, MARCH 20

I had another talk with my father tonight. He feels that it will be safer if I go to live elsewhere—maybe to a place outside the city. I told him I want to go into the woods and join the Partisans. I know he was pleased and proud that I felt that way, but still he put his foot down and said I would have to wait until I was a little older. Sometimes I wish Father *had* left Poland and had taken me with him. Maybe in the West I could have joined the Polish Forces and learned to fight the bloody Germans instead of being stuck here in a house full of old women. All I ever hear is "When you are older." I can only talk about sex when I'm older, I can only live on my own when I'm older, and now I find I can only fight Germans when I'm older.

WEDNESDAY, APRIL 2

Today, to my complete surprise, my old Scoutmaster, Ludwik Berger, came to the house and had a talk with my parents. It is all arranged—I'm to go to his place to live. It's a decision I am excited about so I will pack some things right away and leave this evening. So, parents do sometimes listen to you and respect your wishes! Father really is special, and I am both happy and grateful that he sees I need to get away from this smothering company of old women.

THURSDAY, APRIL 3

Ludwik's apartment is on Czarniecki Street, which is actually quite close to Feliński Street.

My new abode is a small, pleasant room under the roof, with steep-sided walls. Until midday, the sun shines on the writing table, the walls, and the glazed tile stove. Pigeons roost under my attic window and wake me up early with their gurgling, cooing sounds. I miss my own white pigeons, but these will be my friends.

The whole apartment is small. Besides Ludwik, two sisters in their twenties, Stefa and Ola, live here; there is a little boy, Ludwik's son, Marek, who is eight years old; and a tiny old lady, Stefa's and Ola's grandmother. I asked the old lady where Marek's mother was. She told me that Ludwik and his wife had separated some time ago, and the wife lives somewhere out of Warsaw now.

In the apartment also lives a beautiful and very nice Angora cat. I usually prefer dogs, but this cat I think I'm going to like.

FRIDAY, APRIL 4

Ludwik was my Scout instructor before the war, and I still look up to him.

Ludwik is tall, with thick, dark hair. His gaze is sharp, and he looks one straight in the eye. An uncommon bravery shows in his

Ludwik's house, Czarniecki Street

handsome, nervous face. He smiles infrequently, but his voice is commanding, his diction is excellent, and when he speaks it is deliberate and with conviction. He never sits for long, though.

Ludwik generally wears a long, belted coat with a pair of Polish officer's boots, but seldom wears a hat.

I know hardly anything personal about Ludwik. He does not talk much about himself or his family, except the fact that before the war he was connected with the famous Reduta Theater School. Stefa tells me the plays he produced were characterized by fiery patriotism. I think he is a born leader.

SATURDAY, APRIL 5

I met Ola at dinner tonight. Stefa had prepared the meal and said she was sorry there was not more. But Stefa is cheerful, and I like her very much. She treats me like an adult and a friend.

Stefa and Ola are daughters of a doctor and community leader. Stefa is intellectual, while her sister is more the athlete; she used to give physical education lessons at a girls' secondary school. During the 1939 attack Ola showed great bravery in the defense of Warsaw and went into the trenches to help dress the soldiers' wounds.

Execution of civilians

Execution of civilians   *A public hanging*

THURSDAY, APRIL 10

> I am continuing my daily movements around the streets of the city. It seems to be getting more and more congested with German military traffic; I take every opportunity to misdirect this by shifting the street signs. Long convoys are coming through town, and German Military Police are at every major intersection to direct them through the city. I stationed myself on Wilson Square today and when asked for directions, I enjoyed sending the Germans astray, but I hope that soon I will be able to do more to the Germans than waste their gasoline and their time!

SATURDAY, MAY 3

> Third of May Day. Everyone is talking about a speech Winston Churchill made which was heard on the Underground radio. He said:

>> Every day Hitler's firing parties are busy in a dozen lands. Monday he shoots Dutchmen; Tuesday, Norwegians; Wednesday, the French and Belgians stand against the wall; Thursday is the day the Czechs must suffer; and now there are the Serbs and the Croats to fill his repulsive bill of executions. But, always, all the days, there are the Poles.

> If the Allies know this much about what is happening to us, they must be planning to come and help us soon.

The hangmen

THURSDAY, JUNE 5

When I stopped at home today, I overheard Father whispering to Mother about Uncle Norbert. There is a rumor that someone has escaped from Auschwitz, and the news is that Uncle Norbert has helped to organize an Underground group there. Although he is sick and very weak, he is still playing an important role in the Resistance Movement. We hear that the other prisoners are doing everything possible to help him and look after him. I am happy to hear this news, of course, and still pray Uncle will survive. But the way people talk of the dreadful conditions in such camps makes me afraid he will not.

SUNDAY, JUNE 22

All the newsboys have been out on the streets shouting, "Extra, Extra!" I ran out and stopped one of them. He handed me the *New Warsaw Courier.*

HITLER'S PROCLAMATION! the headlines read. FROM THE NORTH SEA TO THE BLACK SEA MILITARY OPERATIONS START TODAY IN THE EAST! And farther on down the news column, "Greatest concentration of armies in the history of the world!"

I ran home with the paper and handed it to Ludwik. He became very excited, exclaimed, "This is the beginning of the end," and left the house in a great hurry.

So now it is the turn of the Russians, and *that's* good news!

SATURDAY, JULY 12

Ludwik and I have had a long talk, and he revealed to me something I had not known before—the existence of a secret military organization, the Union for Armed Resistance (ZWZ). He asked if I would like to join and fight the Germans. I was thrilled and accepted at once, of course.

TUESDAY, JULY 15

Ludwik is preparing me to be an Underground fighter. He introduced me today to the conspiratorial work of the Underground Army, emphasizing the obvious need for total secrecy and discipline and, most important of all, for the willingness to lay down one's life in the fight for freedom. I can't say I really want to die, but I can see now that there are times when one has to be prepared to do just that in order to save others from the Germans.

SATURDAY, JULY 19

This has been one of the most important days of my life. Ludwik came to me this evening and told me to get my jacket and cap and to come with him. Since it was after curfew, we avoided any lighted streets and silently made our way along Czarniecki Street, crossing the wide green swath dividing Krasiński Street, passing through a narrow residential street, and on down in the direction of the Vistula, until we reached the protective cover of the Lower Park near the river's edge.

There, in the bushes behind the dark pines, a number of individuals were waiting for us. The group already seemed to know that I was joining them. To my great surprise, I learned that Ludwik, my sponsor, is their commander.

The ceremony began.

First came the password, "Honor."

Then the response, "Service."

A man came forward, stood to attention before Ludwik, and reported, "Group ready for the oath, Sir."

Ludwik took over the command from him and ordered the group to form ranks. I realized then that I was not the only one about to take the oath.

On the small square between the rows of bushes there was almost complete silence. One could hear only the rustling of leaves, and from time to time the lights of passing vehicles could be seen over the high flood embankment. The orders sounded:

"Fall in."

"Dress by the right."

"Attention."

And then came the solemn order; "Prepare for the oath."

The line stood unmovingly, each man bareheaded and making the double-fingered, eye-level salute. There, in the very heart of the General Government Area—in Occupied Poland—sounded the words of the soldier's oath:

> In the presence of God Almighty I swear that I will faithfully and to the end defend the honor of Poland. I will fight to liberate the country from slavery with all my strength, even to the sacrifice of my life. I will obey all orders of the Union without reserve and will maintain complete secrecy whatever might happen to me.

Then came the response to the oath:

> I accept you into the ranks of the soldiers for freedom. Your duty will be to fight with arms in hand for the rebirth of your country. Victory will be your reward. Treason will be punished by death.

The words of the oath and of the response died away and still we stood motionless, everyone dreaming the same dream: the regaining of freedom and independence for Poland.

The military orders "Company!" and "At ease" brought us suddenly back to reality.

After the order to fall out, the new fighters for freedom dispersed under the cover of night and the protective shrubbery. From that moment, I began my real fight against the enemy.

I returned home with Ludwik, but neither of us spoke.

TUESDAY, JULY 22

I went to the first secret meeting today. I walked up Polish Army Avenue, keeping a watchful eye on everybody who walked behind me. The meeting took place in the house of Lance-Corporal 'Boruta' (Devil), which I reached in midafternoon.

'Boruta' informed us about the rules of secrecy and told us of the basic regulations. We are not to know each other's real names, addresses, or other forms of identity; each of us is to adopt a pseudonym of his own choosing; and we are not, except on rare occasions, to meet others of our group.

The main mission of large parts of the Underground is to train and prepare for the Uprising—to get ready for open fighting. At the moment, direct actions against the Germans are performed by special groups only.

We are to be trained as infantry, with particular attention to city fighting, and will prepare for special work which we will undertake as members of the Couriers' Section. From time to time there will be maneuvers outside the city.

Our section consists of five people, not counting our commander, Lance-Corporal 'Boruta.' His pseudonym suits him very well. Thin, very tall, and round-shouldered, with a hooked nose, he indeed looks devilish! I have taken the pseudonym of 'Chojnacki,' after one of my uncles who was taken prisoner by the Germans in 1939.

Since the choice of a pseudonym is left up to the individual, the way of making such a choice depends upon one's imagination. Some select theirs from history or literature; others use biblical or foreign names, or pick one at random from the names of animals, places, and battles.

THURSDAY, AUGUST 14

We met our platoon commander, Lieutenant 'Władysław,' today; he gave us the details of the company to which we are assigned. The name of our platoon is 'Walecznych' (Brave), that of our company is 'Orzeł' (Eagle), and our battalion is 'Baszta' (Battalion of the General Staff). The company's commandant is 'Michał' (Ludwik), and I have been assigned as his courier.

WEDNESDAY, AUGUST 20

Ludwik is spending a lot of time at the Lower Park. The gardens there border the Vistula, but the river is shielded from view by the high earthern flood embankment. The streets of Żoliborz run down to the Lower Park, which is divided into tiny lots. Each of these is assigned to a family, usually one living in the Housing Co-operatives. They are postage-stamp-sized gardens, but each has a little shed for tools, and sometimes a small bench also.

Families go there on Sundays to work their plots. The soil is rich and sandy and, with a little water, each plot can supplement the family's need for food. Thick red radishes, tomatoes, cabbages, strawberries, anything the family wants to plant seems to grow here.

Down at one end, where several paths meet, there is a large shed where the main implements are kept. As manager of the gardens, Ludwik makes his quarters here. He works here, people know him, and they can verify his identity. He is well liked, it seems.

SUNDAY, AUGUST 24

I was reminded today that the members of the Underground use assumed names only. Thus, if any member is caught, tortured, and breaks down, he can divulge only the pseudonyms.

Ludwik pointed out that this makes it difficult for the Germans to track us down. He also says that it is important for us to maintain our identity papers in absolute order. There are few members of the Underground who do not owe their lives to the fact that they were able to produce proof of legal employment when stopped.

Virtually all members of Ludwik's unit have proof of "legal" employment, and my father has provided jobs and work documents for many of them. Legal cover is essential for civilians and members of the Union for Armed Resistance alike: in our company there are streetcar conductors, secretaries, sewer repairmen, and other City Hall employees. Our colonel is a "garbage man," our major a "bookkeeper," and Lance-Corporal 'Boruta' is a "city fireman."

Ludwik's "passport" shows him in the dress appropriate to the role he is supposed to play—a park supervisor. His identity papers were printed and signed under direct German supervision, and marked with official stamps by the City Hall. I wonder if my father arranged it for him?

MONDAY, AUGUST 25

Ludwik walks the two miles from the Lower Park to Czarniecki Street in all kinds of weather. Today I noticed he did not stride along as usual, but walked more slowly and somewhat stiffly. When he got inside the house, he quickly removed his coat, and from under each arm he took a Colt pistol and placed them on the table. We were all wide-eyed and aghast, even little Marek. We knew better than to ask questions, and he simply said, "Airdrops."

Ludwik has prepared a secret hiding place for them in a space under the floor of the living room, which he showed to us. He is taking a chance, but there can be no secrets here—not even from the curiosity of little Marek.

SATURDAY, SEPTEMBER 20

Autumn is here. Today I went with my mother to Praga; Aunt Zosia had called us to come. There we found five people, a Jewish family from Lwów—Doctor Jan Łoziński, aged about 60; his wife, Zofia; their son, Jan, aged 20; their daughter, Krystyna, aged 24; and Krystyna's husband, Jacek, a physician, aged 28. They are all looking for a place to live, and Aunt Zosia's place is too small. She and Mother have decided to give the spare room to the doctor, and have found a place in the apartment above for the son; the other

85

three went back with Mother to Feliński Street. My mother knows it is not safe for the family to stay in our house for long because of frequent Gestapo searches there, so she plans to find a place for Krystyna and Jacek with some friends of hers in Żoliborz. Then she and Mrs. Łoziński will go to Baniocha.

SUNDAY, OCTOBER 5

Aunt Zosia came to see the family this morning. She was very agitated and told them that, three days earlier, her new "guest" had gone for a walk with his son, Jan. They had been out for a while and were some distance away from the house when they saw two German policemen coming toward them. Jan began running, and the Germans immediately opened fire and shot him. The Doctor managed to get away, and later came back to Aunt Zosia's apartment and collapsed.

The next day, she said, the Gestapo worked from house to house, trying to discover who lived in each one and taking many people with them. They also came to her apartment. Aunt Zosia had been on duty at the hospital, but got back just in time to put Dr. Łoziński in a big chair and cover him with a blanket so that he looked like a very sick, old man. When the Gestapo came into the room, Aunt Zosia, still in her nurse's uniform, told them he had typhus. The Gestapo men left very hastily, without bothering him, but Dr. Łoziński refused to go out again after that.

WEDNESDAY, OCTOBER 15

A messenger came to the house early in the afternoon with a telegram for Aunt Stacha, containing news of Uncle Norbert. It was an announcement of Uncle Norbert's death in Auschwitz. No details were given, not even the date he died. My parents and I are stunned and heartbroken. We had all hoped that Uncle Norbert would somehow survive and be free again. I went to Aunt Stacha in her room, where I found her aimlessly polishing the furniture, obviously still in a daze of shock.

"Uncle Norbert is dead," I said crying.

Aunt Stacha did not respond. Her face was expressionless, and her eyes seemed like empty blue pools. She continued her dusting, moving about silently as if I were not there. I sat quietly for a while and then left, going out alone. I feel as if the whole world is crumbling around me, and I am unable to accept the fact that Uncle is gone.

SUNDAY, NOVEMBER 2

This is All Souls' Day. A friend of Uncle Norbert's came to the house to see my father this evening. The man spoke briefly with my father in the study, then he left.

Father came out, looking pale, holding an envelope in his hand, and beckoned me to follow him to Aunt Stacha's room. He gave her the envelope, which contained a few papers and mementos of Uncle Norbert, together with information that he had died from exhaustion and malnutrition in Auschwitz. At the camp he had loyal followers, but his job in the camp kitchen—which they had given him in preference to harsh outdoor work—had not protected him from the brutalities of life there, and he had passed away on September 21.

I went to the living room and sat at my favorite window. The first snowflakes were falling on the carpet of golden leaves. Winter was making its entrance even before autumn was over, and I felt chilled already.

When the evening lamps began to light up, I noticed people walking past the window carrying small lanterns. The Germans had lifted the curfew for All Souls' Day. I decided to get out of the house and into the evening air, and went to put on my hat and coat. The snow was falling in huge crystal flakes, softly and quietly, upon the people in the streets making their way to Powązki Cemetery.

I made my way up Polish Army Avenue. As I reached the crest of the avenue, I found myself in the crowd of people all going to the Powązki Cemetery. This year there were more souls to be remembered than ever before.

Following the growing crowd, I walked along the avenues and

streets until I reached the wide sidewalk adjacent to the high brick wall enclosing the cemetery. In front of the gate leading into the grounds sat a group of old women in babushkas selling flowers, wreaths, and candles. Thousands of candles, glass-encased to protect them from the gusts of wind, lit the snow-covered paths, each tiny flame a salute to the soul of a loved one who had died.

At the main gate I bought a couple of simple laurel wreaths and made my way to the section of the cemetery where my grandparents' grave was located. I found the carved granite slab and placed one of the wreaths there; the other I carried under my arm as I walked aimlessly among the crowds of people on the pathways.

On my way out of the cemetery I walked alongside the rows of countless simple crosses with steel helmets that marked the graves of the defenders of the city—showing the ranks, regiments, and names of the fallen soldiers. Beside one of them I placed the remaining wreath—for Uncle Norbert. Like the soldiers, he had given his life in defense of his country.

THURSDAY, NOVEMBER 13

Soviet bombers got through the German air defenses of Warsaw today, and dropped bombs in the center of the city. They hit the railroad yards and some apartment houses. Now we are being attacked from the air as well as on the ground!

THURSDAY, NOVEMBER 20

The Germans are moving the Wall, reducing and dividing the Ghetto. Going to church today on Leszno Street, I noticed parts of the old wall torn down. I asked some friends about it, and they said a new wall was going up in this area, making the Ghetto smaller. No one knows what it means, and I think we dread to know.

THURSDAY, NOVEMBER 27

Our field training has begun. This morning about seven o'clock, we loaded up with backpacks and equipment and went to the Warsaw–

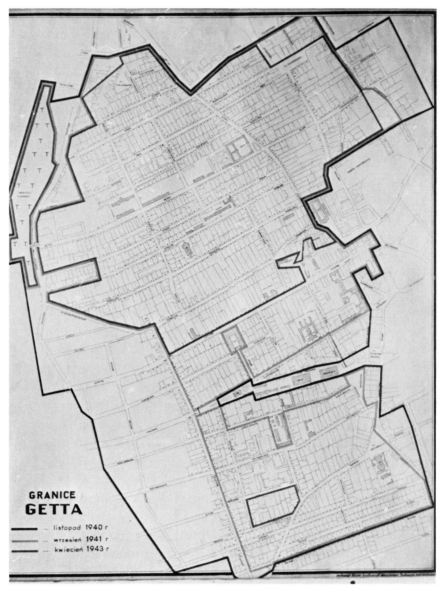

GRANICE
GETTA

listopad 1940 r
wrzesień 1941 r
kwiecień 1943 r

Ghetto boundary, September 1941

Gdańsk Railway Station to wait for the train which would take us to Choszczówka, a little place in a thickly wooded area not far from Warsaw.

We assembled under the station viaduct. The light snow flurries of the night before had stopped, but it was bitterly cold. While waiting for our train we noticed one of the many long troop trains pull in from the Russian Front, which was now frozen near Moscow. As the cars slowed to a stop, a macabre scene met our eyes.

The train seemed strangely silent and no faces could be seen at the wide windows of the passenger compartments. Instead, through the frost-painted glass we saw row upon row of bunks covered with motionless bodies swathed in white—heads in white turbans, arms and legs wrapped in bandages, and propped up or suspended in traction. The frozen bodies of the wounded soldiers, some still wearing parts of their combat uniforms, shook slightly as the train shuddered and stopped.

Even then, with the exception of the stationmaster in a red cap and a couple of white-clad German nurses, no sign of life appeared at the station. Steam from the warm underbelly of the engine emitted a lonely hiss. It seemed that we ourselves became frozen as we watched the ghost train. Then the red flag went up and, with a soul-piercing whistle, the train moved on with its ghostly cargo. We last saw it as it went past the wire-topped wall of the Ghetto.

After that, we boarded our train for Choszczówka and rode in silence to our destination.

When we arrived we went straight to the predetermined meeting place in groups of four, to commence our strenuous training activities—marching, attacking, storming, and scouting the terrain. Through the trees we caught glimpses of other groups going through the same exercises.

At four o'clock we took the train for home. In the gathering dusk the winter landscape moved before our eyes in a slow blur, the train stopping at the many little stations en route to Warsaw. I was repeating the day's roll call of military disciplines in my mind, when my tired body took over and I fell asleep.

MONDAY, DECEMBER 8

Ludwik came home jubilant today. He says that the newspapers are carrying a report that Japan has declared war on Britain and the United States. Now the Germans will have to join their Far Eastern allies, and that will really bring a quick end to the war!

America seems so far away to me—I wonder what the war will be like now. I don't even know what types of ships and planes the Americans and the Japanese each have. I am puzzled as to what the Japanese are thinking of? Surely they can't be strong enough to beat the British Empire and the American industrial power combined?

I asked Ludwik, but he seems to be as puzzled as I am. He did, however, tell me not to worry—there'll still be plenty of chances for me to fight before it's all over. I hope he's right!

SATURDAY, DECEMBER 20

I have come to Feliński Street for a few days, and Mother is back from Baniocha, making preparations for Christmas. There is not much food to be had, although the Germans are giving an extra kilo of bread and three eggs per person for the holiday. Generous of them!

THURSDAY, DECEMBER 25

I am spending Christmas with the family. There are several empty chairs at the table, and everyone is very subdued.

Aunt Stacha refused to eat any Christmas dinner, but she called me to her room and handed me an envelope. She said it was from Uncle Norbert and that she wanted me to keep it in remembrance of him.

After dinner I went to my room and opened the envelope. It was a poem, the last Uncle Norbert had written:

I could quicken death
And run away from the field
Where fear tears apart the last lights—
I wait, however.
Let fate run its course
The soul will not be dishonored
In the ashes of fear.
After my death, from the lonely grave
I wish a bitter flower would grow
And again look proudly
To the clouds of misfortune
To changeable heights
Proving there is not penance
In my coffin.

I am alone!
I cry in vain
Alone and helpless
Like a dried up leaf
The winds of the desert
Are carrying me
I am dying!
Heart, have courage
In this final tribulation.

I felt a terrible tightening in my chest, as though I would burst. Then I wept.

1942

THURSDAY, JANUARY 1

Notices have appeared on the streets and squares of Warsaw. All skis and ski boots in the entire General Government Area must be handed over. One of these notices already has a big "1812" printed over it—we know about the battle fought between the mighty German Army and the Russian winter.

FRIDAY, JANUARY 2

The demand for winter equipment was also printed in today's *New Warsaw Courier*:

> At this moment, our soldiers need skis for their bloody battles with the Red Army, the tool of world Communist Jewry. Your cooperation in supplying the needed skis and ski boots will enable the German soldier to put an end to this threat once and for all. A vicious threat hangs over the head of every child, woman and man in the whole of civilized Europe. . . .

SUNDAY, JANUARY 4

I had to climb over snowdrifts today in the bitter cold on my way to Professor Lewandowski's house on Mickiewicz Street. Passing Wilson Square, I saw a group of people huddled around one of the little coke stoves set up on the squares of Warsaw by the city administration. I found the Professor in his living room wearing a scarf and woolen mittens, with only the tips of his fingers showing. There was no heat in the house, for his meager ration of coal had run out back in December. He had used up the last shovelfuls in keeping warm over the holidays. The Professor greeted me with a smile, and then he took me into the kitchen, where in the middle of the floor were the remains of five pairs of varnished skis. All of them had been cut up into fifty-centimeter lengths.

I had to laugh as I discovered my dignified Professor in the role of prankster. Very clever, too, for now the Germans won't get his skis, and he will have firewood!

THURSDAY, JANUARY 15

Today Ludwik showed me his favorite poem of Krasiński's:

> A voice called in the eternal sky
> As to the world I gave a son
> So to it, Poland, thee I give.
> My only son he was—and shall be,
> But in thee my purpose for Him lives.
> Be thou the truth, as He is, everywhere
> Thee I make my daughter!
> When thou didst descend into the grave
> Thou wert, like Him, a part of human kind.
> But now, this day of Victory,
> Thy name is: All Humanity.

I was surprised but pleased, for Ludwik seldom shares anything personal with me.

MONDAY, FEBRUARY 16

The Underground Press says that General Sikorski has reorganized the Union for Armed Resistance (ZWZ) into the Home Army (AK).

It explains that the Underground Army has reached organizational strength far in excess of that required for mere resistance operations. The new function of the Home Army will be the war of liberation, culminating in a nationwide Uprising.

Ludwik told me that 'Baszta' Battalion, originally just a small group of resistance fighters which he helped organize soon after the campaign of 1939, has now become a major unit in the Home Army, with a full complement of three companies. Of the three companies, Ludwik is the commander of one, our company, 'Orzeł,' and he says that our military training activities will now be much more frequent and intense.

Ludwik spares no effort to purchase arms from German and Ukrainian supply sergeants, with funds provided by the Home Army. These arms, together with weapons received from airdrops, are stored in secret caches throughout Żoliborz.

The company is growing—new sections, new detachments,

96

new platoons, and many new recruits. Until now our company had consisted of those who had been in Ludwik's prewar Boy Scout units. Now it includes many in their late teens and early twenties, but we are all equally in great need of military training. I hope I don't let them down—and I'm determined to show them that the younger boys can fight as men.

FRIDAY, FEBRUARY 20

I saw Mother today. She told me Father was asked by the Underground if he would not leave on a plane which would pick him up and take him to London. Father again refused. He feels that he can best serve the Polish cause by staying in Poland.

SATURDAY, FEBRUARY 21

It is cold, cold, cold. Stefa has told me that she saw a sign on the statue of Copernicus in front of the "Blue" Police station, stating he was a German. What gall!

TUESDAY, FEBRUARY 24

I had lunch at Feliński Street today. On the way back I saw a new announcement on Wilson Square, signed by Fischer and saying that "hooligans" had removed the sign on the Copernicus statue. In retaliation, Fischer has ordered the statue of Kiliński on Krasiński Square to be taken down.

SATURDAY, FEBRUARY 28

Poor Father—with all his problems of trying to save as many lives as possible, and countering German repressive measures, he is now having to battle with the Germans to preserve the city's monuments, which they are threatening to destroy. (The one exception is the Kiliński statue, which they have put in the basement of the National Museum.) We Poles have always been proud of the heroes of our history and heritage, and destroying our monuments would be a severe blow to morale.

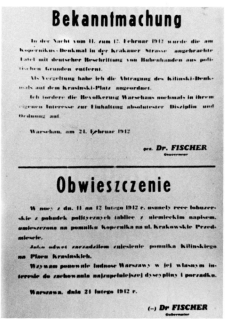

Fischer's order for removal of the Kiliński statue from Krasiński Square

Statue of Kiliński

TUESDAY, MARCH 3

I celebrated my thirteenth birthday today, and Father managed to spend some time with me. He tells me that he has received a direct order from the *Wehrmacht*—all city statues are to be melted down. Father has been to see Leist, who is mad that the *Wehrmacht* is giving orders without consulting him. He is so furious, in fact, that he has given my father permission to go ahead and have casts made. Father said to me with a smile, "It's going to take months, maybe years!"

TUESDAY, MARCH 31

The food situation in Poland is awful, and the Germans are taking everything. Now there is nothing more to sell, and my mother is resorting to bringing in sacks of potatoes and sugar from the country, riding in crowded trains, and looking out for police patrols when approaching stations. If she sees a patrol, she has to throw the precious food out of the window in order to escape arrest and deportation to a concentration camp. I am very proud of the way Mother is standing up to wartime life, but then I probably used to underestimate her.

MONDAY, APRIL 6

Mother has told me more of the efforts being made, particularly by the women, to provide food for us. Smuggling of food into Warsaw is largely done by women like my mother. They smuggle bacon and other food wrapped up and hidden under their clothes, or hidden in suitcases and handbags, for use by their families. Professional smugglers, on the other hand, transport between one and two hundred kilograms of food in secret hiding places in the railroad cars— below the floors, behind the walls, and even in the engine compartment itself. There are also a few large-scale smugglers, both within and outside the Ghetto. In collaboration with bribed Germans, they smuggle food by train and truckload into the city, and even into the Ghetto. These few are making fantastic fortunes out of the misfortunes of others.

A street search

THURSDAY, APRIL 16

I went to town to see the results of these efforts for myself. There are a few large Black Markets in Warsaw, the most famous being the one at Kerceli Square. There, among the hubbub, droves of men mill around the wooden kiosks offering food and supplies at exorbitant prices. In spite of the profits, this is a dangerous business, for the square is often surrounded by armed police who confiscate all the articles, destroy and burn the kiosks, and catch the smugglers and deport them to Germany. All of this is to little avail, however: next day, among the smoldering ruins, new kiosks and new salesmen replace those of the previous day.

The street-corner trade is carried out from lightweight baskets, which the vendor grabs and carries off when given the signal that a German police patrol is approaching. The signal usually comes from outlook posts manned by children who sell Black Market cigarettes.

Individual German soldiers also participate in the Black Market. Airmen or soldiers on their way to the Russian Front sell wines, liquors, and cosmetics for large profit. Ludwik buys radio transmitters and weapons from supply sergeants. We know that some German soldiers will sell anything for a price.

Many of the senior German officials responsible for the distribution of food on the official market sell it instead on the side. Those caught are usually punished, but the Black Market continues.

THURSDAY, APRIL 30

Ludwik says that the situation in the Ghetto is getting worse. There the rations are one-third the size of ours, and the prices are even higher. Food is thus totally beyond the means of the poor, who literally starve to death in their homes and on the sidewalks. Inside the Ghetto in general, the situation has reached crisis point. Stefa insists that the Germans want to let the Jews die of starvation.

Hunger

SATURDAY, MAY 2

Tomorrow is our national holiday, the Third of May, a decisive moment in the annals of freedom, our "Magna Carta." Father has taught me that it goes back to the eighteenth century, when the Constitution of the Third of May, 1791, was declared. This Constitution abolished serfdom, ended the feudal system, and granted human rights to all citizens.

The Constitution of the Third of May, according to Father, also restored political rights to towns and citizens. The townspeople, who had been disenfranchised for about two centuries, were given back the rights and privileges until then held only by the *szlachta* (the gentry). To celebrate this day, Ludwik has ordered our company, now consisting of about two hundred men, on a three-day military maneuver in the Great Kampinoska Forest. Fully armed and partially uniformed, we are to start out after dusk from Bielany. We will then march in small groups for some five hours to our meeting place. I hope my boots hold out.

SUNDAY, MAY 3

We are now in a part of the Great Kampinoska Forest, northwest of Warsaw and south of a bend in the Vistula. This particular part of the forest stretches for about thirty-five kilometers in an east-west direction, and at its deepest point it covers about fifteen kilometers. The thick primeval forest is full of natural wildlife, with some swampland. There are a few small villages, but otherwise it is uninhabited, and it provides a perfect place for our partisan activities.

Ludwik, the chaplain, and the battalion doctor drove in style to Kampinos in a captured Opel, with Lance-Corporal 'Boruta' as the driver. However, this bravado nearly cost them their lives. Passing through a small country town, under cover of night, the car's engine conked out—unluckily right in front of a German military barrack. The Germans opened fire without asking questions. Ludwik set the car on fire and, under the rain of bullets, escaped with his three companions. They reached our positions after an hour's marching, exhausted but jubilant to see us all there and to be alive themselves.

After their arrival there was a parade and then we all went to a field-Mass. The solemn service inspired us, as we started our mock attack. In detachments and platoons, running and dodging, we advanced until we had covered three kilometers.

Nearly dead with fatigue, we found ourselves before a hill occupied by the "enemy," and we started to storm this objective. With shouts of "Hurrah, with bayonets!" we lunged forward to take the hill. Everybody was excited, and some of us began to fire our pistols and machine guns in the air. When I saw the leader of our detachment shooting with his Sten gun, I could hold back no longer. Like the others, I began to fire my precious ammunition in the air from my V*is* pistol.

The shooting could be heard all over the area, and when it stopped, Ludwik approached us in a fit of anger. He sternly reprimanded us, ordered a meeting and, as a punishment for shooting without an order, temporarily suspended all ranks. It was the worst punishment that could have been inflicted upon us, for it will prevent us from "fighting" for a whole fortnight. I am really mad at myself for breaking discipline like that.

MONDAY, MAY 4

Thirsty and tired from our continued march today, we drank from road puddles and swamps, as there was no clear water anywhere. Ludwik gave us an hour's rest and then ordered us on another march which did not end until the evening.

TUESDAY, MAY 5

At dawn today we were on the march again, by now pushing ourselves far beyond our strength. A little way along the road we saw a few German Military Police approaching on bicycles. They quickly disappeared from view when they noticed us; we left quickly ourselves—we weren't going to be around when they returned with reinforcements.

This afternoon we returned to Warsaw, some almost crawling on hands and knees, inhumanely tired and dirty, and now beginning to realize what it's like to be a soldier.

WEDNESDAY, MAY 6

Another Underground organization, probably the Communists, has attacked one of our magazines. Our few guards were terrorized, and quantities of arms and ammunition were stolen.

The Polish Government-in-Exile in London is sending arms to the AK (Home Army) and not to the AL (the Communists). The Russians, tied down on the Front with the Germans, are not yet able to form a strong Communist Underground. There is no love lost between us and the AL, for the AK takes its orders from our Government in London, while the AL's orders come from Moscow.

THURSDAY, MAY 7

Ludwik is furious about yesterday's raid. After talking with other officers, he has posted guards at our magazine. He has information that the thieves are likely to come back for the remainder of our arms tonight.

Another platoon has been detailed to help us, and this caused an unfortunate accident. The leader of our platoon, Second Lieutenant 'Władysław,' after placing guards, went to inspect the sentries and to see that the observation posts were in order. Unfortunately, he went to a post consisting of members of the other platoon, who did not know him. Perhaps 'Władysław' made a quick movement or the guard was just too nervous—nobody could ascertain quite what happened—but three bullets were fired from a Colt .45, striking the Lieutenant in the chest and killing him instantly.

FRIDAY, MAY 8

Ludwik has given me a very sad mission to perform: to take an official document to the parents and brother of the officer who died yesterday. His brother happens to be Lance-Corporal 'Boruta.'

MONDAY, JUNE 1

Today Ludwik sent me with a coded message to 36 Twarda Street, near the Little Ghetto. He told me the place where I was to deliver the paper was the office of a dermatologist. The room I entered had a floor-to-ceiling glass case full of jars, bottles, and flasks, containing various creams, solutions, and lotions. I was welcomed by a nurse in a white uniform, who took the message after the exchange of passwords. She told me that the Doctor was in the surgery and said good-bye. I wonder what the message could have been about? But I'm sure the Doctor must be a high-ranking member of the Underground.

FRIDAY, JUNE 5

This evening Ludwik talked with me about the possibility of being caught by the Gestapo and what I should do in case this happened. If stopped with a copy of any coded message, I must roll it into a tiny ball and swallow it. If arrested, I am to tell them that I know nothing about any Underground activity. As far as my relationship with him is concerned, I should tell them that I know Ludwik only as my Scoutmaster. In general, I should take the attitude that I really cannot stand him, for he is dictatorial and prevents me from doing what I want. In other words, I should play the role of a spoiled brat.

SATURDAY, JUNE 6

Today I asked Ludwik more questions about what I should do if I get caught. For example, do I try to break away?

He says that my responsibility as a soldier is always to try to escape. If I cannot, and if I am stopped with any incriminating materials on me, I should not give myself up alive if possible. When I have a weapon, I should use it, but I should reserve the last bullet for myself.

He advises me to learn self-defense tactics, such as kicking one's opponent in the groin or jabbing one's fingers in his eyes. I wish I could put these tactics into practice right now!

WEDNESDAY, JUNE 17

Today Ludwik and I went to the park. We talked about the Russians and the Germans and an Uprising. He said that if the Soviets succeed in turning the tide and reentering Poland, we may very well again face two enemies.

I said that I was interested only in fighting the Germans because they had taken our freedom from us. "No more than the Russians," he answered.

Then I asked him to tell me about the Uprising, whether it would be like a regular war, or like the partisan battles?

Ludwik thinks that it will be something halfway between regular war and armed revolution.

He reminded me that the Uprising must be preceded by a long period of preparation, and a very detailed and precise plan of action. The first attacks of the Uprising, in order to be successful, will have to be extremely intense and widespread.

He said that we are going to have specific objectives to attack, and that during those hours each platoon and each company will be pretty much on its own. Ludwik does not know how many of us will live to see that day, but hopes he will have the privilege of leading all of us when the order comes.

WEDNESDAY, JULY 1

I met my mother and sister this afternoon at Inwalidów Square; we were going to visit Aunt Zosia in Praga. As we stood waiting for a streetcar from Bielany, my sister jumped up and down with excitement at seeing me; in the old days she and I never stopped fighting, but now with my being away from home it was different. She had even let my mother hold her favorite doll, although she was also hanging onto Szkut, our dachshund.

A little boy in rags came up to us and began to sing a ditty:

> When a German puts his foot down
> The soil bleeds a hundred years;
> When a German drinks water
> The well rots a hundred years;
> When a German breathes three times
> There will be a hundred years of disease;
> When a German offers his hand
> It is the end of an agreement,
> Because everything bothers him
> When it is not within his power.

Ragamuffins make their living this way, and I gave him the few coins I had.

Suddenly, a newsboy approached us from the direction of the Warsaw–Gdańsk Station. In a voice stressing urgent news, he called out, "Manhunt, Manhunt—Attention, Attention!" and he was gone. I looked around and there were the green uniforms of the German police.

"*Halt, Halt, Hände Hoch!*" was enough for me to push my sister into the nearest doorway and up a steep staircase. My mother followed with Szkut. At the top, panting for breath and from fear, I pushed the apartment doorbell. A woman opened the door, and we pushed past her. We told her that there was a manhunt going on in the street, and she took us into a small back bedroom. We

A street arrest

all stood in silence looking at one another, but Szkut barked and my mother had to hold him to quiet him down. We heard the sound of trucks starting up and then silence. The old lady looked at my mother, and said fearfully that before the war it was stray dogs that were hunted in the streets and driven off in vans—now it was the turn of the humans.

WEDNESDAY, JULY 8

I went over to Feliński Street to see my parents today. Father says Czerniaków visited him again in his office this morning. Czerniaków bluntly asked whether my father knew the fate of Jews being deported from Warsaw. Father told him he fears it is true they are being taken to their deaths, that there no longer appears to be much doubt about that. He felt Czerniaków would want to hear the truth, for they have worked together closely since 1939. Czerniaków told my father he doubts that either of them will survive the war. I hope Father doesn't think that too.

107

SATURDAY, AUGUST 1

I have not seen Zula for a long time, and the news from behind the Wall is bad. One hears gruesome accounts of the starvation and deaths in the Ghetto, and I feel totally helpless. Today I went to see my old history teacher, Mrs. Bernardyńska, and took a copy of a back issue of the Underground newspaper. The article on the front page described the conditions behind the Wall. After my teacher had locked the door, she sat down beside me and we began to read the news together:

> Poverty, hunger, cold, and appallingly unsanitary conditions have created a monstrous situation. In one house on Miła Street, occupied by five hundred people, two hundred sixty-six have died so far. At 63 Pawia Street, where seven hundred ninety-four people lived, four hundred fifty have died, two hundred during the last month. At 21 Krochmalna Street, occupied by two hundred people, all have died. . . .

Mrs. Bernardyńska wept and trembled as she read those figures. I put my arm around her, then she said, "I cannot read anymore. I have so many friends there."

I left her and went back to Czarniecki Street, where I finished reading the paper:

> In these conditions, the death rate in the Ghetto is enormous. During 1941, the reported deaths by month were:

January	898	July	5,550
February	1,023	August	5,560
March	1,608	September	4,545
April	2,601	October	4,614
May	3,821	November	4,801
June	4,290	December	4,966

> A total of 44,277 people, or 10 percent of the population, died during 1941.

Who knows how many have died *this* year?

A Ghetto child

SATURDAY, AUGUST 8

I have learned that Mrs. Bernardyńska tried to kill herself after I had read the paper with her. Luckily, her daughter went to see her that day and found her mother in time. She took Mrs. Bernardyńska to Child Jesus Hospital, where I am going to visit her.

THURSDAY, AUGUST 20

Soviet bombers from Russian bases have appeared over Warsaw, hitting the railroad yards and some apartments in the area. They bring feelings of hope, mixed with fear and anger—hope because this means the Front is now pushing toward Poland; anger at the further destruction of the city; and fear because the daily attacks and arrests by the Germans on the ground are now compounded by possible death by the Russian bombs from the air.

TUESDAY, SEPTEMBER 1

Ludwik came yesterday and told me that he was going on a mission into the Ghetto and that he wanted me to go along; in case anything happened to him, I was to return and make a report to our company. I wondered just what he thought might happen to him, and why it wouldn't happen to me too. However, I felt I couldn't press him for details at this time, and certainly didn't want to let him know I was actually pretty scared at the whole idea.

In the early hours of the morning he took me to a house, very close to the Wall. We were met inside the house by a young man who was to be our guide. In order to preserve the secrecy of the route in and out of the Ghetto, we were blindfolded and literally led by the hand as we silently went downstairs to the cellars and made our way through a series of narrow, interconnecting underground passages.

After we had stumbled along for what seemed like hours, our guide stopped us and removed our blindfolds. When we had adjusted to the daylight, we saw that we were inside the Ghetto near Miła Street. Our guide then handed us over to two other young men who were to escort us to the actual meeting place, but first

Inside the Wall

Starvation

they took us into a building nearby and made us change into rags like theirs—our clothes were in too good a condition and would have betrayed us in an instant.

The sights in the Ghetto were unbelievable. People moved like skeletons—scarecrows with sunken, glassy eyes. The dying lay on the ground or leaned against the buildings. The stench of the de-

111

composing corpses, and of the living, was appalling. That walk was a living nightmare. There did not seem to be any old people, yet everyone was old. The sight of the children, silently begging and dying before our eyes—their bones sticking out of their rags—was so pathetic as to be unreal. No prior description of conditions inside the Ghetto had prepared us for this reality.

As we walked along those streets, people suddenly started to run past us. Around the corner of Zamenhof Street came a solitary German soldier, firing at random. Our guides dragged us into a doorway, as he sprayed the street with bullets. The first to fall was a woman, shot in the stomach, then two men fell bleeding to the ground. The soldier, seeing that the rest of his targets had managed to get away, then turned back down Majzels Street. I had heard rumors that soldiers on leave often came to hunt starving Jews on the streets of the Ghetto, but I had not really believed such stories until now.

Deportation

Our guides had lived in the Ghetto long enough to be outwardly unmoved by this experience, but I could see that Ludwik was horrified by what he had just seen. I was numbed. I just couldn't take it all in.

We were now late for our meeting with members of the Jewish Underground, who got down to business as soon as we arrived. A young man told us:

"Our intelligence unit has gathered the following information on the present status of Polish Jews in Warsaw. We want this transmitted to London immediately. Prior to the mass deportations our population had reached about four hundred thousand. The first order for five thousand people a day came in July. Supposedly they were being sent for work in the country, while actually they were transported to extermination camps.

"The Germans give every starving volunteer who reports for deportation at the *Umschlagplatz*—near Stawki Street—three kilograms of bread and one kilogram of jam. The forewarnings of the leaders go unheeded. Starvation takes the upper hand. The argument, 'They would not feed us if they planned to kill us,' is enough. In any case, those who do not go voluntarily are brutally herded onto the trains, shouting and crying."

They also told us that on July 23, in a desperate attempt to warn his people, Adam Czerniaków had written a note, "Three P.M. So far, three thousand ready to go. By four P.M., according to orders, there must be nine thousand. I am helpless; sorrow and pity fill my heart. I cannot stand it any longer. My end will show everybody what must be done." He had then killed himself.

Ludwik broke the silence, "Did the people get his message?"

"The news of Czerniaków's death spread like fire. It was a clear-cut warning of the liquidation of Warsaw Jews. However, even now, most people refuse to believe the truth. The smell of fresh bread wins them over; its sweet aroma tempts their starving bodies and confuses their minds. Hundreds gather at the *Umschlagplatz* every day, waiting for the train; some days there are two trains, and twelve thousand leave."

"What is the population of the Ghetto now?" Ludwik asked.

"Our latest reliable figures show one hundred thousand."

113

"What happened to the others?"

An older man spoke for the first time, "According to our confirmed and most reliable reports, all Polish Jews deported from Warsaw have been murdered, mostly in gas chambers at Treblinka. One of our intelligence officers spent a few days there disguised as a Lithuanian SS officer. He reports that it takes half an hour to gas four hundred people; he also says that up to forty gassings can take place in twenty-four hours, although this is exceptional. The daily average is five thousand people.

"Most of the deportees from Warsaw are taken directly to the gas chambers upon arrival. Only those who cannot be liquidated on the day that they arrive are taken to the barracks. Corpses from the gas chambers are cremated in specially constructed rooms, bones being removed from the back of the ovens and placed in crushing machines.

"There are other methods also. One is packing people in a cattle wagon, with quicklime covering the floor. Water is then pumped in and the cars sealed. When they are opened up later, those occupants who have not been burned to death are shot.

"Another method is pumping carbon monoxide into the trucks. But most die in the gas chambers in Treblinka."

Ludwik, who looked as sickened as I felt, said, "I will report this word for word. Is there anything else that you want and need us to pass on?"

The younger one spoke again, "Yes, and it is this. We feel that the only solution is the one we have proposed to the United States and to the Government-in-Exile in London. We have suggested that the Polish Government insist that the Allies take similar steps against German citizens or citizens of German origin in those countries, in retaliation for what is happening to Polish Jews here in Warsaw.

"The Polish and Allied Governments should inform the German Government of this policy of retaliation. Germany should know that, for the liquidation of Jews, Germans residing in America and in other countries will have to answer. We realize that we are asking the Polish Government to advocate unusual measures, but it is the only way to save millions of Jews from certain death. We know what has already happened to three hundred thousand Jews in Warsaw.

"We also know, of course, that such action probably cannot be taken, but at least our request will bring attention to the plight of our people."

WEDNESDAY, SEPTEMBER 2

Ludwik and I spent the night in the Ghetto but said very little to each other, and the meeting resumed this morning.

The younger man spoke, "What we need now is arms and ammunition, so that we can start an Uprising. We know that we should have been training as your Underground Army has been doing, and I do not want to waste time discussing why this has not happened. But the Germans have unified us by their uncontrolled aggression; we are determined to fight, and we need every bit of help we can get. We intend to defend every last brick in this part of Warsaw.

"We know we cannot win, but we want to die as fighting men rather than slaughtered animals. We are the conscience of the Jews of the world, and if we die, we will die fighting for the future of the Jews."

On the way back to the Aryan side, we saw posters warning people that if they boarded the trains it would mean their going to the extermination camps.

The posters pleaded:

> HIDE YOUR CHILDREN, HIDE YOURSELVES!
> RESIST DEPORTATION!
> JOIN THE RESISTANCE!
> DON'T DIE WITH A TORAH IN YOUR HAND—
> DIE WITH WEAPONS IN YOUR HAND!

WEDNESDAY, SEPTEMBER 9

I can't shake off the memories of the Ghetto. At night, the ghastly events and sights of a week ago march before my eyes again. During the day, wherever I look I can still see the nightmarish sights. I

115

Death Train

Call to fight

can smell death all around me. And yet I can't really absorb what I've seen. I can't understand, comprehend, or believe. I keep asking myself how it could happen, and why it continues.

There must be more that can be done to help. I shall have to talk to Ludwik.

THURSDAY, SEPTEMBER 10

Ludwik says that just about everything that can be done is being done. Almost every Jew who has escaped from the Ghetto has either been taken into hiding here or given refuge somewhere in the countryside. The 'Żegota' (Jewish Assistance Unit), an arm of the Underground, is increasing its efforts to get more people out of the Ghetto, but it is a slow and dangerous process. Yet Ludwik fully understands the depths of my despondency, and he shares my frustration.

Meanwhile, he has passed on the information we were given in the Ghetto, and assures me that the arms requested, and promised, are being sent.

Yet even this seems inadequate, and increases our feelings of helplessness.

We can understand the Jewish Fighting Organization's reluctance to leave the Ghetto and join forces with us, and yet there seems to be no alternative.

THURSDAY, OCTOBER 8

Every day we have been expecting Soviet bombers to hit Warsaw in force, in advance of the Front moving westward. Last night I thought they had come, for heavy explosions woke me up. The explosions seemed to be in several parts of the city. At breakfast I asked Ludwik about it. He does not think they were Russian bombs but the actions of the Commando groups. He had heard they were planning to derail trains moving tanks, planes, and ammunition to the Eastern Front. I envy them these actions!

WEDNESDAY, OCTOBER 28

I have been instructed to transport guns and ammunition from one of the most recent airdrops to the Fire Brigade Building. Ludwik supervised me and three other members of our company in delivering the precious cargo from our secret cache on Czarniecki Street to the officer in charge of Hook and Ladder Unit No. 2.

The idea is to hide the arms underneath the fire-truck equipment, and send it into the Ghetto this way the next time the Germans order the truck into the Ghetto to fight a fire there. Ludwik will make arrangements to notify the Jewish Fighting Organization as soon as this happens, so that they will know when to expect the delivery and will be ready to receive it.

This is one of the best ways for us to get arms inside the Ghetto and to make certain that the right people get their hands on them.

So finally, I have a chance to participate in fulfilling the promise Ludwik made during our mission to the Ghetto last month.

Żoliborz Fire Brigade Building, Słowacki Street

Żeromski Park, Żoliborz

SUNDAY, NOVEMBER 29

Ludwik called a meeting of our entire company tonight in Żeromski Park. It was a brisk, cold night, as Ludwik and I slipped out of the apartment after curfew. We entered the park through an opening cut in the chain-link fence which separates our garden from the park. Ludwik walked quickly, as usual, and I had a hard time keeping up with him. No words passed between us.

In front of the park benches not far from the exit to Wilson Square, the entire 'Orzeł' Company already stood in military formation. I joined my section, while Ludwik stopped in front of the company and proudly surveyed us. One of the platoon commanders came before Ludwik, saluted, and reported the company ready. Ludwik issued the orders "Attention" and "At Ease."

Then solemnly, in a clear and resonant voice, he addressed us:

> We are gathered here today to celebrate the night of November 29, 1830, when Cadet-Officers from the Military School fired the first shots at the Occupier. These shots for freedom can still be heard today. As we prepare for the moment of reckoning with today's Occupier, the deeds of those young Cadet-Officers take on a very special meaning.

119

We stand united against all terror and oppression
and, as in days gone by, our battle is for freedom. Our
fight is a universal one—we are opposed to any form
of tyranny and stand ready to defend our freedom with
our lives.

Then Ludwik began citing the names of our comrades who
had been killed during the year. This was the first time we had
heard a full list with their pseudonyms and ranks. When he finished, Ludwik ordered a minute's silence in their memory.

As we again stood at attention, in solemn silence, lost in
thought, and extremely moved by this somber occasion, the blackness of the night was suddenly pierced by blinding lights from
trucks coming down the slope of Słowacki Street.

The lines began to break, as everybody instinctively started to
run. Ludwik's command froze us all, "Stand—do not move!"

The lights of the trucks continued to pass over us and finally
the beams of the last one moved on as it passed the boundary of the
closed park. We had to readjust our eyes to the darkness that once
again enveloped us.

Ludwik wasted no time in regaining control. He continued,
"All graduates of the Officer School, step forward."

Now he talked to those who had finished the Underground
Cadet-Officer School, praising them for work well done and wishing them good luck in leading their men in battle. Then he described our visit to the Ghetto and told of the struggle there. Having finished that, he ordered the company dismissed, and we all
vanished into the surrounding trees and bushes.

SATURDAY, DECEMBER 12

Ola is back after a long absence. She will not speak of where she has
been or of what she is doing, but she implies there are going to be
some strong Underground reprisals against top German officials—
not just in Warsaw but in the seat of the German Occupation in
Cracow.

1943

FRIDAY, JANUARY 1

The Germans have covered the city with printed announcements around the Wall and elsewhere. They are signed by SS General Krüger: ANYBODY WHO HELPS JEWS WILL BE SHOT!

SUNDAY, JANUARY 3

The Underground Press responded today with an appeal to the people of Warsaw:

> The Germans have again declared a death sentence on anyone helping Jews to escape or assisting those who have already succeeded in escaping. Every decent person must regard such threats with disgust! To render assistance to our brethren, to save our fellow human beings from extinction, is a responsibility stronger than death. It is the honorable duty of every Pole to help all victims of German oppression.

THURSDAY, JANUARY 7

I have not seen my family since Christmas, which we spent simply and quietly, but happy at least to be alive and together. However, this morning since I was near Father's office and wanted to hear some family news, I went to see him. After the usual wait, I went in. There was no special news from him, but Father confided to me that the day before he, with a group of representatives of the Polish population, had been summoned to a meeting at the German Labor Office, at which Governor Fischer had made a speech. He had a copy of it on his desk:

> Every day, the enemies of the Reich cause untold damage in this city. Every day, Germans die on the streets of Warsaw. We do not take reprisals because we believe that these acts of sabotage are the works of Communists and Jews hiding outside the Ghetto. You must realize by now that the great armies of the Reich are defending the world from Communism, that we are defending the Poles and their freedom. The Poles

are slow to help us in our historic mission. You *can* help us, and should do so willingly by volunteering to work in Germany, so that our soldiers can carry on the fight against the Russians. These workers should come forward without delay. In the next three weeks we need fifty thousand workers to volunteer to come and work in the Reich. It is well paid work and the living conditions are good.

I called this meeting today because I want to issue a joint appeal signed by both of us—you as representatives of the population, and by ourselves—to show mutual understanding of our historic mission to destroy Communism and its threat to the world. We want you to encourage workers to join in our mission by going to work in the Third Reich.

My father told me that he had had to reply on behalf of the Polish representatives and he had said:

Every day, Poles are killed. They are taken to Pawiak Prison and executed. Every day, Poles are hunted on the streets and taken to concentration camps on cattle trains. All this is common knowledge. It is well known that the conditions faced by our people in Germany are terrible. What is known of the situation here in Poland and in Germany will not help your appeal. What I demand is that you release Poles from concentration camps, and that you drastically improve working conditions in Germany. Only after this has been done can you expect any change of attitude on the part of the Poles. Signing a joint appeal for volunteers will not produce results. The people will know that the signatures were not given freely, and I for one will not sign any such appeal.

My father told me he thought that, after his refusal to help the German Labor Office, he too would be imprisoned and would disappear, suffering the same fate as his predecessor and friend, President Starzyński.

MONDAY, FEBRUARY 15

Heavy snow covers the city. Our Commando execution squads have carried out the sentence against a collaborator, Lieutenant Święcicki of the "Blue" Police—sentenced to die by the Underground Court for assistance in carrying out street hunts.

WEDNESDAY, FEBRUARY 24

On the way to a meeting of our detachment today, I saw on Wilson Square the latest proclamation spelling out details of the boundaries of the all-German district of the city. The Germans are beginning to feel the need to close ranks.

THURSDAY, FEBRUARY 25

Ludwik took me to one side today and told me that, for security reasons, he has had to select a new pseudonym again. Two years ago he changed from 'Goliat' to 'Michał'; now he is 'Hardy.'

SUNDAY, FEBRUARY 28

I had arranged to meet Krysia, a new friend of mine, at a corner of Lublin Union Square. Half-frozen in the icy wind, we ran alongside the barbed-wire fencing past pillboxes and sentries who now guard the newly established German residential section.

So, finally the Germans are showing real fear of us! It has taken more than three years' struggle to accomplish this, and I was beginning to doubt that it would ever happen.

And yet here is real proof that the Germans, too, are afraid.

Still they think that they will terrorize us into submission through daily executions on the streets of Warsaw. How stupid they really are! Why can't they see that their terror tactics only reinforce our will to fight back.

WEDNESDAY, MARCH 3

Ola returned today, in time to help me celebrate my fourteenth birthday. She is more confident and defiant than ever. She seems more radiant, with blonde hair and wearing a lot of makeup. Like others, she has been forced to change her pseudonym and identity. She says she is now 'Władka' and is rather mysterious about it. I learn that she has a crucial job—Commandant of the Underground Mail and leader of the long-distance women couriers of the Home Army's General Staff. She is now "unclean"—carrying with her documents of an incriminating nature and sometimes weapons, thus exposing herself to great danger. Ludwik and Stefa were both quite subdued at dinner, and they didn't even tease me about the various girls I have been seeing lately.

SATURDAY, MARCH 6

Ola has finally told me something about the 'Osa-Kosa' Commandos. They are a crack combat group—the nucleus of the Polish Underground Commandos, whose major responsibilities, Ola said, are to harass the enemy through progressively stronger sabotage, to undertake reprisals for acts of violence against the civilian population, and to train men and women for combat action during the coming Uprising.

Ola has been part of 'Osa-Kosa' from the start. Many of the orders for liberating our political prisoners now pass through her hands.

MONDAY, MARCH 8

We are all together again, and I am happy to be "home" with my friends. When Ola got back tonight she was quite animated and pulled from beneath her coat a heavy package which she carefully placed on the dining room table.

"Don't touch that!" she commanded.

We gathered around her in silence and waited to see what she was going to do.

Ola unwrapped the package slowly and produced two little *Wańki-Stańki* ("stand-up bombs")—so-called because when put

126

down they automatically stand upright. There had been three of them, she said, and they were produced by the Underground. The first one had just been tested in a wood near Warsaw; it had exploded instantly on contact with a tiny twig on one of the trees. These two were in her care, and she was awaiting orders as to their use.

WEDNESDAY, MARCH 10

Ola is acting very strangely. On streetcars she travels in the front section, reserved for Germans, thus taking more risks than ever. I have learned that she is also going around under a German name and carrying false German identity papers that have been furnished by the Underground.

FRIDAY, MARCH 12

I have heard little from Ola herself of what she is doing, but have been told by 'Lot' much of what it entails.

At the end of last December Ola had carried an order from the General Staff in Warsaw to the Cracow group of 'Osa-Kosa,' instructing them to start preparing for reprisal action against the Head of the SS and Police in Poland, General Friedrich Wilhelm Krüger. Krüger came to Poland as Himmler's right-hand man in 1939, and was quartered with Governor General Hans Frank in Cracow's Wawel Castle, the ancient seat of the kings of Poland.

At first, the planned reprisal action was to be directed against Frank, but because of Krüger's personal responsibility for the extermination of the Polish Jews and the terror perpetrated by the Occupier upon the whole civilian population, he became Underground Poland's target for reprisal. A detailed plan for the attempt on Krüger's life was being developed, and in the meantime Ola was given the order to transport the *Wańki-Stańki* bombs to Cracow.

WEDNESDAY, MARCH 24

Our Commandos today achieved a new victory: after a fierce battle, they succeeded in freeing twenty of our captured Freedom

Fighters from the heavily guarded armored vans transporting them between Szucha Avenue and Pawiak Prison.

SATURDAY, APRIL 3

Ola left home this evening. She did not tell me where she was going, but she was carrying a large leather bag and I guessed it must be a journey of at least several days. Thus, I suspected that she was on an important mission.

In order to make sure that nobody tailed Ola, I followed her at a reasonable distance as she made her way to the Warsaw Central Station. It was the only one used by the Germans on furlough. Day and night trains would leave—in one direction full of jubilant, celebrating Germans going home, and in the opposite direction the silent wagons of those going to the Russian Front.

It was now a few minutes after 10:00 P.M. The platforms were full of gray-green-uniformed soldiers of the *Wehrmacht*, heavily laden with bursting backpacks. Within this human anthill, the dark uniforms of the tall SS officers clearly stood out. Among the uniforms of various ranks, colors, and shades, there were also groups from the foreign legions—softly humming Ukrainians, black-booted Latvian and Estonian SS regiments, and stocky Russian peasants in German uniforms—a real military melting pot!

Ola boarded the Cracow Express at 11:00 P.M. I stood back from the crowd in the shadows and watched as she entered the compartment. Inside were two golden-haired officers with the glittering death's head and crossbones embellishments on their uniforms, who immediately jumped up to help Ola with her heavy overnight bag. Having placed it carefully on the upper rack, they politely seated her opposite themselves.

The officers' attempt to engage the lady in conversation proved fruitless. Giving them a polite smile, she took off her hat and sank back against the soft seat. The two disappointed young men sat back, as if resigned to a conversation with each other only.

Ola was traveling with the identity papers of a German national, Evi Keller. Wrapped in silk underwear in her hand luggage were the two *Wańki-Stańki*, with extra-strong explosives. Ola's unwillingness to engage in conversation with the two SS officers was more than a pretense at being aloof—she spoke little German, and her accent would have betrayed her anyway.

MONDAY, APRIL 5

Ola took the night train back to Warsaw, arriving home at dawn and saying nothing of her trip.

SATURDAY, APRIL 10

'Lot' came bursting into the apartment this evening—judging by the noise he made, he must have come up the stairs three at a time. He waved a copy of the newspaper at us, and was very agitated. When we asked him what his wild behavior meant, he just pointed at the paper which he had flung on the kitchen table, but said nothing.

The front page carried a huge black headline: GRAVES OF POL-ISH OFFICERS DISCOVERED BY THE GERMAN ARMY AT KATYŃ NEAR SMOLEŃSK. The Germans are proclaiming this a Russian war crime against humanity. Probably this is another piece of German propaganda, yet we fear the worst. I am worried sick about Uncle Juzek, and about Zula's father.

The last two pages of the paper carried the names and ranks of officers whose bodies have been exhumed and identified so far; the paper also mentions that they will publish more names, as more graves are opened and the bodies identified.

SUNDAY, APRIL 11

I went over to see Father today, to try and find out more about Katyń. He said that the dead officers all seem to be those captured in September 1939 by the Red Army. He doesn't seem sure whether the officers were killed by the Russians, as the Germans claim, or whether this is indeed another German propaganda smoke screen. However, he told me that Leist had asked him for names of Polish doctors—the Germans want to send them with the international Red Cross team being sent to Katyń to carry out an investigation into the massacre.

129

MONDAY, APRIL 19

Warsaw has been stirred by a monumental event! At dawn today, the Jewish Underground Army started the Uprising of the Warsaw Ghetto by attacking a more than 800-strong group of *Waffen* SS which penetrated the silent fortress under the cover of a tank, two armored cars, and a group of Jewish policemen. The tank was set aflame, several SS men died in the battle, and the Germans withdrew defeated.

Jürgen Stroop overseeing destruction of the Ghetto, 1943 Uprising

At 8:00 A.M., SS *Brigadeführer* Jürgen Stroop, newly named by Krüger as head of the SS and Police for the Warsaw District, took command of the Battle of the Ghetto. While the German artillery started its murderous fire, the Jewish Underground Army raised Polish and Jewish flags above the rooftop of an apartment house on Muranów Street.

130

Ghetto poster

131

In the evening the sappers of the Warsaw Commandos, under Captain 'Chwacki,' were given an order to blow an opening in the wall of Bonifraterska Street opposite Sapieżyńska Street in order to provide direct access to the besieged fighters.

Approaching Bonifraterska Street, the group started firing at the German troops guarding the wall. Immediately, German rein-

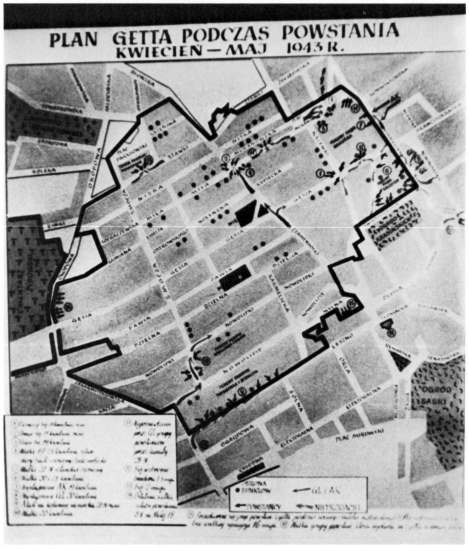

Plan of Ghetto during the 1943 Uprising

forcements came running from the direction of Krasiński Park. A pitched battle ensued, and it soon became clear that it would be impossible to reach the wall against such overwhelming odds. Two members of the group were killed in the battle, 'Orlik' and 'Młodek.' Three others were seriously wounded.

'Chwacki' ordered a retreat and the unit withdrew in the direction of the Vistula. As they withdrew, they saw the Germans tending to their casualties. We hear that the first day of the battle cost the Germans more than one hundred lives.

Rooftop sniper

TUESDAY, APRIL 20

A group of Jewish Freedom Fighters today waged a bitter battle on the opposite side of the Wall from where the Commandos had attempted *their* attack. With hand grenades, firebombs, and mines, they defended themselves against the attacking units of the SS under the personal command of Stroop. Rumor has it that the General Staff of *Żydowska Organizacja Bojowa* (ŻOB) rejected the German ultimatum to lay down arms and surrender, passed to the Freedom Fighters through the Jewish Council. After that, the Germans brought tanks, field artillery, and armored cars into the battle.

133

Captured Freedom Fighters, 1943 Uprising

Since I was assigned as a messenger on Bonifraterska Street, I could see for myself the battle being fought on both sides of the Wall.

I found myself in the midst of the crowd on the sidewalk. Amazingly, every time a streetcar passed alongside the Ghetto, both sides—Germans and Freedom Fighters alike—held their fire. I simply could not believe my eyes. It was certainly the most unreal battle I could imagine.

About 3:30 P.M., when the streetcar to Bielany was waved through the fighting, I saw a burst from a machine gun topple three Germans, the crew of a field gun positioned to the right of the crowd. As if with one voice, the crowd cheered the Freedom Fighters' success, the women crying with joy, and the men shouting words of encouragement.

The Germans, furious, turned their guns on the crowd, and people scattered.

The whole city has been revitalized by the action of the Freedom Fighters, and some of the churches have arranged special services to offer prayers for them.

I wish we could get the order for a full-scale Uprising!

WEDNESDAY, APRIL 21

Two hundred and thirty Freedom Fighters have died in the Ghetto. The Germans are systematically destroying house after house, but are paying a bloody price for each captured bunker. This entire section of the city is enveloped in heavy gray and black smoke, and the glow of the fires consuming the buildings can be seen from every part of Warsaw.

THURSDAY, APRIL 22

The *Luftwaffe* today joined in the uneven fight, sending *Stuka* dive-bombers from Bielany airfield and systematically dropping incendiary bombs upon the insurgents. The flaming inferno increases in intensity with each day. The Germans seem clearly determined to burn all the inhabitants alive and to reduce the Ghetto to ashes. In the meantime, the head of the Jewish Fighting Organization, Mordechaj Anielewicz, has written in a letter mailed outside the Wall to his second-in-command, who is with us:

> . . . only a few individuals will survive, and the rest
> will be killed sooner or later. The future has been set;
> in all bunkers occupied by our soldiers it is now impos-
> sible even to burn a candle because of the lack of air.

At noon Commandos attacked the Germans outside the Wall. Led by 'Stadnicki,' the unit attacked and killed SS police units guarding the Leszno Street gate. Simultaneously, a group of Commando officers attacked Germans on Okopowa Street. Captain 'Szyna' killed a number of German officers entering through the Gęsia Street gate in a police car.

Captured Freedom Fighters, 1943 Uprising

FRIDAY, APRIL 23

Warsaw has been greatly moved by a large poster freshly pasted on a signboard on the corner of Bonifraterska Street:

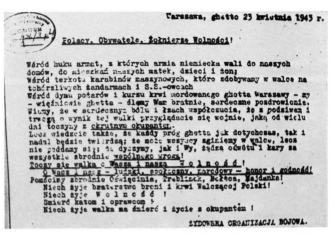

For Your Freedom and Ours!

(WARSAW—THE GHETTO, APRIL 23, 1943)

POLES, CITIZENS, SOLDIERS FOR FREEDOM!!

Amid the deafening noise of the shells which the German armies are pouring onto our houses—the homes of our parents, families, and children;

Amid the reverberations of the machine guns which we are capturing in battles with the cowardly SS men and military policemen;

Amid the smoke of the fires, the dust and the blood of the murdered Warsaw Ghetto:

We, the prisoners of the Ghetto, send you brotherly, heartfelt greetings. We know that you are with us in the battle which for many days now we have been waging with the cruel Occupant—sincerely sharing our pain and shedding tears of sorrow, with admiration but with fear over the results of this fight.

But, know also that every corner of the Ghetto, just as each has been up to now, will remain a fortress; that maybe all of us will die in the fight, but that we will never surrender. Know that we breathe, just as you do, with wishes for reprisals and punishments for all the crimes of our common enemy!

The Fight is being waged for Your Freedom and Ours!

For Your and Our Honor and Dignity—Human, Social, National!

We will take retribution for Oświęcim [Auschwitz], Treblinka, Bełżec, and Majdanek!

Long live the brotherhood of arms and blood of Fighting Poland!

Long live Freedom!

Death to the executioners and torturers!

Long live the fight for our life and for death to the Occupier!

JEWISH FIGHTING ORGANIZATION

SATURDAY, APRIL 24

In the midst of what is going on in Warsaw, I have heard about what happened in Cracow from Ludwik's friend 'Lot.'

On April 4 the head of the Warsaw 'Osa-Kosa,' 'Jurek,' arrived in Cracow with a written order. This order from the Underground Court condemned General Krüger to death; the sentence was to be carried out "promptly."

Wawel Castle, Cracow

138

April 21 was Adolf Hitler's birthday, and that morning a high-ranking officer was seen on the escarpment of the Royal Castle, overlooking the Vistula. He was on his way to attend the Führer's birthday celebration, and was picked up at the uppermost gate of Wawel Castle by a shining gray Mercedes touring car. The car slowly made the descent down the twisting, cobblestone drive.

The car reached the bottom of the hill and passed Bernardynów Square, then gained speed and hastened along the bank of the river and on to Krasiński Avenue.

At the junction of Wygoda Street in front of the depot of the Cracow SS, a group of workers was attempting to dislodge the enormous roots of a huge tree stump. Just then they noticed two youths, each with a pot of red and white tulips in his hands. The mustachioed foreman shrugged his heavy shoulders and muttered, "Birthday, my ass!" Then he continued pulling at the stump along with his men.

'Stanisław,' stationed at the end of Wygoda Street, raised a handkerchief to his nose to notify 'Góral' and 'Jędrek' of the approaching car. It was about 10:00 A.M. Against the background of Dębnicki Bridge they saw the approaching Mercedes. When the car was in range, 'Stanisław' signaled, "Throw!"

Both flowerpots landed in the back of the car, and an enormous detonation shook the street. As swirling smoke covered the pavement, 'Góral' fell to the ground but 'Jędrek' remained standing. The explosion blew the windows out of the SS building; cobblestones flew into the air and left two gaping craters; the car veered and stopped in the gutter.

Shots were fired and 'Stanisław' ordered the retreat. While 'Jędrek' was running along Wygoda Street, a German soldier came out from a building and tripped him, but a shot from 'Stanisław's' gun felled the German. The Commandos then separated.

The Germans announced later that the assassination attempt had failed.

We do not know what to believe. It seems to me that it might be another German propaganda trick. After all our planning we surely couldn't have failed to kill that butcher!

However, in spite of myself I feel very uneasy, and pray that my doubts will prove unfounded.

Ghetto roundup, 1943 Uprising

Death march

The end of hope

The Wall

MONDAY, APRIL 26

General Stroop has reported that more than one thousand Jews have been flushed out of the bunkers and that they were immediately liquidated. In addition, several hundred were killed in battle, and the Germans also captured many Jews who maintained liaison and worked with the Polish "terrorist" groups. At the same time the General Staff of ŻOB has sent out its last communiqué:

> The number of men, women, and children lost in the fires and by execution squads is enormous. Our final days are approaching. But, as long as we have weapons in our hands we will continue to fight. . . .

TUESDAY, APRIL 27

Cinders and burned papers cover the streets of Żoliborz. Ludwik and I talked today about the situation. From the apartment, we could see only the dark southern sky; and to get a better idea of what was happening, we took a walk. After crossing Inwalidów Square we climbed up the Warsaw–Gdańsk viaduct.

Below us lay thick clouds of smoke. Explosions reverberated behind the Wall. As we stood there, the wind changed and the sweet, putrid smell of burning human flesh was in our faces. The flames, spurred by the breeze, shot higher, and the bottom layers of the cumulus clouds boiling over the Ghetto turned from amber to red.

The whistling sound of jets of air created by the diving *Stuka* bombers was the only other noise. Artillery barrages in these last days of the Ghetto had almost stopped, but squadrons of *Luftwaffe* planes continued to drop incendiary bombs upon the already airless, flame- and smoke-choked Inner City.

It seemed so pointless with the destruction already so complete. Yet the incendiary bombs kept falling, each one giving birth to a new tongue of flame which shot through the gray and black

The Oppressors

The final hours

smoke clouds. The Germans were carrying out with cold precision the Führer's order to complete "the Devil's work" in Poland.

Anger welled inside us. To be inactive at a moment like this made us sick at heart. To make it worse, as we slowly descended the viaduct, a convoy of light tanks and mechanized fire-throwers passed, heading in the opposite direction. On the vehicles sat smiling, flaxen-haired members of the SS "Blood and Ashes" Brigade.

Everything that Ludwik could do had been done to help the Ghetto. Further action was now impossible. Talk was grossly inadequate, and what was happening was eating our hearts out.

On the way home we stopped and sat in silence and subdued spirits on a bench in Żeromski Park.

WEDNESDAY, APRIL 28

A group of Cadet-Officers under the command of 'Szrapnel' have successfully attacked SS guards on Zakroczymska Street, but the entire Ghetto is now in flames. The Germans have shut off the city water supply and the Ghetto is burning totally and helplessly, but *Heinkel* bombers still systematically drop incendiary bombs, while renewed barrages of artillery fire pour thousands of rounds, at close range, into the buildings.

The final hours

THURSDAY, APRIL 29

With the Ghetto burning, the Germans in other parts of the city are trying to divert our attention.

I was riding back to Żoliborz today and the streetcar was crowded. Next to the barrier on the open part of the streetcar I watched the fragments of the city; the color of Warsaw seemed gray. Somehow the gray streets, houses, streetcars, and parts of walls all looked the same.

When I got off at Wilson Square I saw a large crowd gathered before a big movie screen. A huge, open grave was being shown; German soldiers carried bodies out of the grave on stretchers and placed them on wooden tables. By the tables stood officers from many armies. Among German doctors and *Wehrmacht* officers, I spotted a number of Polish officers from 1939 in full uniform. Others wore American and British uniforms. They must have been prisoners of war brought from German camps to Katyń, which was near Smoleńsk. The scene changed, and on another set of tables were displayed the mementos found on the bodies of the executed officers—the *Virtuti Militari*, the Cross of Valor, documents, letters, military caps, belts, and other items taken from the graves in order to identify the dead. Clerks were sorting the documents and passing them to the Polish Red Cross workers.

143

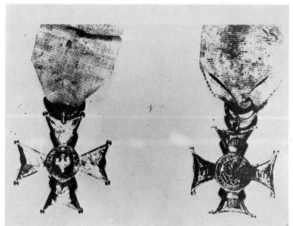

*Katyń massacre relics from Polish officers:
(top) insignia and personal effects; (left) medals; (right) a cap badge*

The voice from the screen described the horrors of this un-precedented murder of thousands of prisoners of war. It then stated that the families of missing officers ought to read the *New Warsaw Courier* in the days and weeks to come, in the hope of find-ing the names of missing fathers, brothers, and uncles. If they did, they should go to the nearest office of the Red Cross to obtain fur-ther information and to collect any mementos.

When the film was over, I heard two city sanitation workers ar-guing, "Jacek—I tell you, Germans do not shoot men in the back of the head with individual pistols. They use machine guns."

"And I tell you, Kazik, who the hell except the Germans would shoot unarmed men gagged and tied like pigs?" My mind was in such a turmoil after what I had just seen, that I didn't know what to think as I walked back home, but I did fear for Uncle Juzek.

SATURDAY, MAY 1

Krüger, who escaped the attempt on his life in Cracow, today vis-ited the battlefield that was once the Ghetto. I bet he is happy with the destruction but embarrassed that the fighting still continues. After all, Berlin must be awfully mad that the elite SS troops have not yet put down the Jewish–Polish Uprising.

MONDAY, MAY 3

I went to church this afternoon with Danka and Basia, twin sisters who live in the Glass House apartments near Wilson Square. Al-though the church was crowded and full of flowers to mark our Na-tional Day, people were in a somber and fearful mood. More can-dles than ever were burned for the departed.

SATURDAY, MAY 8

The Germans today surrounded the bunker at Miła 18 in the Ghetto. Among the leaders who were trapped in the headquarters bunker was Mordechaj Anielewicz. Rather than fall into enemy hands, he committed suicide.

SUNDAY, MAY 9

Word has reached us that a handful of survivors have left the ruins of the Ghetto through the sewers. We understand they left yesterday, but so far we have no further news of them. I wish I could get news of Zula too!

MONDAY, MAY 10

At 10:00 A.M. today, the cast-iron sewer cover at the corner of Prosta and Twarda Streets was pulled off, and a group of Freedom Fighters came out—incredibly, some still carried weapons—in front of astonished passersby. They were loaded into two waiting trucks of the Underground Army and taken to the woods outside the city.

SATURDAY, MAY 15

Details of the Ghetto survivors' escape through the sewers have now become known. We understand the group comprised about forty people; slipping and falling in the fast-moving slime, they had to scramble over barbed-wire barriers and crawl flat under suspended hand grenades. Some people were so crazed with thirst they began to drink the sludge and died soon after in extreme agony. When the remaining survivors reached their destination point, they had to wait there for thirty hours before it was safe for them to climb out.

SUNDAY, MAY 30

Through a report smuggled to Ludwik, we have learned that at dawn yesterday five hundred men and twenty-five women were taken to the courtyard of Pawiak Prison. In groups of about thirty, they were then packed into closed trucks, and transported to the burned-out ruins in the depths of what a few days earlier had been the Warsaw Ghetto. There, they were lined up in rows against the charred black wall. Machine guns, manned by regular German SS troops and Ukrainian support units, were ready. There were long bursts of machine-gun fire, and the first row went down; then

146

the second, and the third, until the twisted, bleeding corpses were all that remained. The bodies were then dragged along the ground and stacked on wooden funeral pyres by the Ukrainian troops. After dousing the human remains with gasoline, they set the stacks on fire.

Prisoners in Pawiak were overcome with nausea from the putrid smell of burning flesh.

"The Devil's Work" (Hitler's words)

SATURDAY, JUNE 5

Another of our couriers has reported that a marriage took place today in the Church of Saint Aleksander on the Square of the Three Crosses. The service started at noon. The bridegroom, Mieczysław Uniejewski, was a Lieutenant in the Polish Navy and had escaped from a prisoner-of-war camp in Germany. He was now an active and popular member of 'Osa-Kosa'; the bride was the pretty Teofila Suchanek. Both had invited their families and friends, among whom were many prominent members of 'Osa-Kosa.' One of them was Ola Sokal ('Evi Keller').

While the service was under way, police trucks—"kennels," full of helmeted German SS police—thundered onto the square from the adjoining streets. Troops with machine guns quickly surrounded and entered the church. Inside, the first person to notice the commotion was the white-clad priest, who at that moment was reciting the part of the marriage ceremony which blessed the young couple. Without changing the tone of his voice, he said, "We are surrounded. People, do not lose your heads. Pray."

He had just spoken these words when more armed Germans came through the doors, pointing their guns at the frightened people, and shouting, *"Hände hoch!"* Searched, pushed, and handcuffed, the prisoners were then herded down the aisles and out onto the square, where they were locked into the "kennels." Minutes later, at Pawiak Prison in the heart of the burned-out Ghetto, Gestapo agents found something incriminating on several members of the wedding party.

Only a collaborator, a traitor, could have given them such a windfall.

Altogether, some eighty-nine people were taken to the Prison. The bride arrived at Pawiak still clutching her bouquet of small red roses. Among the fifty-six people the Gestapo kept in jail were Ola and the Gestapo's collaborator—the "V-Man," or *Vertrauungsman*.

The only ones who escaped arrest were 'Andrzejek,' the bride's brother, and 'Balon,' who had left to purchase some film shortly before the ceremony began. A lucky few also escaped at the last minute by jumping unnoticed into the church catafalques.

THURSDAY, JUNE 10

I learned today from an Underground source that the prisoners taken from the church were led through the courtyard of Pawiak Prison for interrogation. On the way they were marched in front of a window, behind and to the side of which stood the collaborator, pointing out certain individuals from the wedding group to the Gestapo. The "V-Man" was a medium-sized fellow, thin, with a swarthy complexion and jet-black hair. While identifying the members of 'Osa-Kosa,' he hid his face in his hands.

FRIDAY, JUNE 11

Now that we have heard about Ola's arrest with the other members of the wedding group, Ludwik has decided it is better for both him and me to leave the house for a time. He left first, packing a few things hastily and going out through the back garden into Żeromski Park just as it was getting dark. As he said good-bye to Stefa, I felt very sad for them both; she looked so small and frail, he so worn and distracted, already a hunted man. I left shortly afterwards, going in the opposite direction, up Czarniecki Street and on to Wilson Square before making my way back home to Feliński Street.

FRIDAY, JUNE 18

I ran into Ludwik in Bielany today, at the tram station. We walked for a few minutes together, and he gave me some details of the fate of the wedding party. With the exception of the bride and her parents, who were sent to Auschwitz, he has been told that almost all of the group were executed in the ruins of the Ghetto. Among them were the two members of 'Osa-Kosa' who had thrown the bombs at General Krüger's car in Cracow. Ludwik knew nothing about Ola, and he was obviously too upset to even talk about her.

WEDNESDAY, JUNE 23

Stefa rang me this morning and asked me to come over as soon as I could. Her call was a welcome break, and I went at once. But the news that awaited me could not have been worse.

Stefa was pale and looked more frail than I had ever seen her. She spoke in a whisper, and what she said was mixed with tears.

From Ludwik's intelligence contacts she had heard about Ola. When she was arrested at the wedding, Ola had some "mail" and her false identity card with her, positive evidence to the Gestapo of her Underground connections. She had been taken with the others to the Gestapo Headquarters in Szucha Avenue shortly after the arrest. There, under interrogation, she had refused to answer any questions. Neither threats nor beatings could break her.

When these tactics failed, the interrogators began to kick her with their boots. Other tortures, human- and machine-inflicted, followed. Little pieces of wood were driven under her nails, and later, she was put on the rack, the "bed of death." By the time that last session of interrogation and torture was over, Ola had apparently felt she might finally break and betray her comrades. So, back in her cell she had reached for the cyanide pill concealed in her clothes. Aleksandra Sokal—beautiful Ola—thus remained silent until the end.

Grief and pity overwhelmed me, as Stefa finally broke down and wept—only she could know the full bitterness of such tears. We don't even know the exact date of Ola's death, but believe it was June 20.

WEDNESDAY, JUNE 30 AFTERNOON

After hearing about Ola's death, I remained at my parents' home on Feliński Street, but I kept in touch with Stefa. As nothing more happened, I returned to Czarniecki Street today.

After lunch I expected a friend of mine to visit me, but he did not come. Stefa sat with me but spoke very little. She was sad and apprehensive—Ludwik was in hiding; Ola was dead; and Stefa herself was living on borrowed time. Little Marek was in the room, playing with his toys on the floor. He seemed her only consolation.

At three o'clock a knock came. I asked, "Who is it?" and a voice answered, "Friend."

I started toward the door to open it, but Stefa stopped me. She whispered, "Don't move." Then she said loudly, "If you do not identify yourself, I shall not open the door."

The reply was a harsh shout: "Gestapo! Open the door or I will shoot through it." Stefa went to obey, knowing she had no choice.

At the same moment, without thinking, I ran to the next room and tried to open the window to jump out. I was too late. I heard a peremptory *"Hände hoch!"* and turned to see the muzzle of a machine gun aimed at me. I raised my arms, positive that all was lost, and quite frankly scared stiff.

Still holding his gun, the Gestapo man turned me toward the wall and searched me from head to toe. Other Gestapo men entered and began a rapid search of the house. I knew at once they were looking for two things: Ludwik and arms.

I stood still, giving a sideways look at Marek. He caught my glance and quickly turned away toward his toy menagerie in front of him on the floor, as if unaware of the drama around him. The Gestapo men in their long leather coats assembled in the living room. They ordered Stefa and me to leave, but two of them stayed behind with Grandma and Marek.

As we left the room I looked back and caught one last glimpse of little Marek. He was sitting right over the secret trapdoor to our arms cache, talking to his toy family spread out on the carpet. Then he looked up at me, and as the sunlight fell upon his face, I saw tears forming in his eyes. It was the last time I would ever see him.

They took Stefa and me down the narrow hallway and outside to a couple of open police cars. In each was a driver and two Gestapo men with machine guns pointing outward. They drove swiftly to the center of the city, to Szucha Avenue, that terrible place where so many Polish fighters for freedom have met their fate.

After an hour at Szucha Avenue, where they completed the dossier on us, they took us in a van under convoy to Pawiak Prison.

WEDNESDAY, JUNE 30 EVENING

Pawiak Prison is situated in the middle of the mined and burned-out Ghetto. The miles of the Ghetto Wall remain reasonably intact after the bombings, but the entire area is under strictly enforced quarantine. I saw no signs of life except for a few German guards, and the whole vast area was wrapped in a strange calm. I caught glimpses of the desolation as we passed through the grim streets before entering the outer gates of Pawiak, and my first thought was that I now had to admit, even to myself, that Zula must be dead.

The first thing I saw as we approached these gates was a pack of wild, lean creatures baring their fangs behind a steel wire fence —German police dogs. The van passed quickly on through the second and last gate, and stopped in front of the reception center. They separated us, taking Stefa to the women's part of the prison and me to the men's section.

Before they led us away, however, we had to line up with our faces to the wall; I moved my hand a little and was smashed on the head by a prison guard so that my nose hit the wall. Stars appeared before my eyes, and my nose started bleeding; but the physical pain did not hurt me as much as the fact that I was quite powerless to retaliate. I realized that what little freedom I had had on the streets of Warsaw hours before was shattered, and that I was now totally at the mercy of the SS guards of Pawiak Prison.

The cell into which I have been put is a tiny one, but I have plenty of company; some of the prisoners are suspected of being of Jewish descent. They consist of unlucky people who were caught in ever-increasing police hunts on the streets of Warsaw, among them an elderly man and a waiter from the Bristol Hotel who talks of his many women.

The old man, dressed in black tails and patent leather shoes, has been arrested for "love"; the police caught him as he was leaving his mistress's house. Judging by his clothes, he must have been out dancing. There is an unwritten law in Warsaw that dancing and similar entertainment are unpatriotic.

Another man in the cell was arrested with his nephew, Zbyszek, who claims he is the son of a millionaire banker. The seventeen-year-old youth was going to the country in an open *droshka* with his mother and uncle, when a policeman stopped them just outside the city. Suspecting that they were Jews, he took them to Szucha Avenue. The youth, who is really spoiled, cries all the time and infuriates us by asking every five minutes, "Uncle, when do you think they will let us go?" It is all he ever says.

WEDNESDAY, JUNE 30 NIGHT

After a medical inspection this evening, they confiscated the few precious things I had on me, including a silver ring made out of a five-*złoty* piece with the crowned Polish eagle. But the worst of the indignities was the forcible shaving of my head.

I have now been thrown into one of the underground cells where virtually all the occupants are common criminals.

The walls and the floors are of concrete and drip with dampness. The cell is about two meters wide by three meters long. There is a small window at the top with strong bars, but it is so high that only a tiny ray of light can enter. The cell is thus in perpetual twilight.

The other prisoners are three middle-aged men and two youths. They are professional criminals. The oldest of the men, with a dirty stubble on his face, is a cattle thief and keeps swearing at his bad luck in allowing himself to be caught. The two youths are brothers who lived near the Ghetto ruins; they had stolen furniture saved from fires and then sold it in the city. They think their trade is a perfectly legitimate one and cannot understand why they have been arrested; after all, they say, the furniture was Jewish. They are a new breed of Poles to me.

The guard has given us a single straw mattress; it is barely long enough for all of us to use as a pillow, and we have to lie down on the wet concrete. We are so cramped for space that all six of us have to turn over at the same time. Nobody can sleep because of the lice which started to crawl over us like an army on maneuvers soon after it grew dark.

FRIDAY, JULY 2

Last night was another sleepless one, disturbed by the cries of the beaten and tortured, the shots of the execution squad, and the moans of the dying. Reveille was at five o'clock this morning, and at six o'clock came inspection. Everybody has to stand to attention inside the cell, when the head prisoner reports in German: "I obediently report cell number ——— with ——— prisoners, all present." If he does not say this correctly, he is smashed in the face; if he gets it right, his reward is the slamming of the iron door. In our cell I am the only one who can speak German, and so I am to have the "pleasure" of reporting for the cell each morning.

SATURDAY, JULY 3

At seven o'clock we get breakfast. It consists of one slice of dry dark bread and half a cup of sour, black *ersatz* coffee. After breakfast, everybody listens anxiously from behind the door as the list is read of those who are going on to Szucha Avenue for cross-questioning. Everybody wants to get out of the cell as soon as possible, even if it means going there, but I have to confess that in spite of all I've heard I have only a blurred idea of what Szucha Avenue really means.

Lunch at noon means a cup of wormy cabbage or beet soup, and we get bread and coffee again in the evening.

Cell corridor of Pawiak Prison

154

SUNDAY, JULY 4

We all have such violent stomach upsets now that we cannot even eat the bread or drink the coffee. This stomach illness is common, but we are allowed to use the "little cowshed" at the end of our corridor only twice a day, and then for no more than ten minutes at a time. Since this is not enough, a corner of our cell has become a latrine.

We have all added our names to the many inscriptions and signatures on the wall of our cell.

WEDNESDAY, JULY 7 MORNING

This morning, a week after my arrest—a week which has been a timeless eternity—I heard my name read from the list of those going on to Szucha Avenue.

At eight o'clock the Germans took me out of our cellar to a waiting room upstairs. There, while standing facing the wall, I turned my head a little and noticed Stefa standing in a row of women on the opposite side of the room. She had seen me too and began to signal to me with her hands.

I turned my head more in order to see her better, and did not notice a Gestapo man coming through the opposite door. He approached me from behind and hit me so hard that I staggered against the wall. Stefa cried out; he shouted at her.

I recovered my senses and bit my lips because of my complete helplessness; as before, that hurt more than any physical pain. After half an hour or so they took us out into the courtyard. It was the first time I had had a chance to see it properly. The prison was surrounded by a high wall reaching nearly to the second floor, and tautly stretched along it were high-tension wires. There was a sentry box about every twenty-five meters.

The van in which we were being transported was nothing more than a big iron box without windows, and with only a small opening at the back crossed by iron bars. We were followed by an open Mercedes carrying six Gestapo men, each of whom had a machine gun in hand ready to fire.

On the way, Stefa and I whispered to one another to ensure

155

that we would give similar answers to the questions which we might be asked. She reminded me of Ludwik's "contingency plan" in the event of my arrest: I was to tear him down as a person, to detract from his importance, and to hide my real connection with him. Stefa and I then said good-bye with the unspoken feeling that it was for the last time.

The van to Szucha Avenue took a roundabout route, in an effort to avoid interception by Home Army Commandos. When we reached our destination, the Germans pushed us out of the van and took us to what they call a "sanitorium."

There are three rooms alongside each other, opening onto a wide corridor. On both sides of a center aisle are rows of chairs, with their backs to the corridor. A prisoner sitting in one of these chairs can see only the backs of those sitting in front.

No one is allowed to move or speak. A Gestapo man walks back and forth, and if anyone makes the slightest noise, he is either beaten with a long rubber stick or is ordered to do sit-ups in the aisle until he loses consciousness.

Adjacent to the three cells was a room which seemed to be occupied by someone who was being beaten. From this room I could hear thuds and screams, and this made me very scared, for even the loudspeaker in the corridor, which blared German and Ukrainian music, did not drown the cries. From time to time, a Gestapo man put plates of steak and fried potatoes on the table in the middle of the corridor, and the aroma played havoc with my stomach. About 11:30 A.M. one of the Gestapo men came to me and asked me to what profession I belonged. When I answered, "I am a student," he took me to the corridor, sat on a chair, and ordered me to kneel and clean his long, dirty military boots. When I had finished one pair I had to clean the boots of two more of these thugs. I was seething with humiliation and anger.

WEDNESDAY, JULY 7   AFTERNOON

After I had finished, they locked me in the "sanitorium" again until early afternoon. Then the Gestapo man who had arrested me came in.

Jackboots

He took me up to his office on the second floor, and there another Gestapo man was waiting. It was a moderately big room with two filing cabinets, two desks, and a few chairs.

I was shaking as I entered the room. My nerves were completely out of control, but I struggled to get hold of myself and not disgrace myself in the presence of these German thugs.

I was ordered to sit in front of the two Gestapo men, who stared straight at me. One of them was playing with a pistol.

First, I was asked if I knew German. I said "No," hoping to gain time between answers while they translated their questions into Polish.

They showed me Ola's false identity papers and asked if I knew her. I answered that the face in the photo was familiar, but that the name on the papers was quite unknown to me. They showed me a large album of photographs and ordered me to examine them and say if I knew any of the people.

I turned the pages slowly. From them, the faces of Freedom Fighters looked out at me. Among them was Ola, together with one of her friends, and other familiar faces. I hope some of them are free.

Looking through the pages I stopped at one of them; "I know this one," pointing at the photo with my finger. The man sitting next to me, thinking he had got something, asked, "From where?"

"It is one of my fellow prisoners, and he is in the cell next to mine, and therefore I know him." The man's face flushed in anger, and I realized how foolish I was to speak so impudently.

When I had looked through the entire album, the Gestapo man changed his tactics. He talked to me in a fatherly way, trying to get me to believe that he knew everything about me, and that because of my youth, if I would tell him the truth, I would be freed. He promised to let me go if I would tell him who brought me into the Underground Army and what company I belonged to.

I answered categorically that I did not belong to any secret organization and had never even heard of any such thing. He cross-questioned me, threatening and pleading alternately. Then he took a piece of paper and typed something. Question began to follow question, as he took down my answers.

"Tell me everything you know about the people you live with. Name everyone who visits the house."

Then he ordered me to separate various papers in a file, with labels such as AK (Home Army), PPS (Polish Socialist Party), PPR (Polish Workers' Party), and "Polish National Party," "Partisans," "Paratroopers," and many others.

I did so, and the Gestapo man gave me the paper with my answers and told me to sign it.

He then started to ask detailed questions about Ludwik. "Who is he? Where does he work?"

During this questioning, I mentioned that Ludwik was the caretaker for some gardens near the Vistula. The Gestapo man went to a map of Warsaw hanging on the wall and began to examine it carefully. He could not find the gardens on it, so he ordered me to help him. A small black square in the middle of the area occupied by the gardens on the map indicated there was a structure of some sort there.

The Gestapo man noticed it and asked me what it was. I told him that it was a shed for gardening tools. Actually, our company's stolen Opel had been hidden there.

The Gestapo men suspected something. They told me to sit down and get some rest, for in a few minutes I was to go with them to the shed; they wanted to see for themselves what was in it. As they told me this, I was petrified, but I struggled to maintain an outward calm.

I tried to persuade them that it was a waste of time, as I knew there was nothing there. They ignored me, and we then all got into an open car marked with the infamous "POL," meaning police. There were three Gestapo men in the car with machine guns, pistols, and hand grenades; they told me that they had orders to kill me if I tried to escape.

WEDNESDAY, JULY 7 EVENING

As we entered Marszałkowska Street, a main artery of Warsaw, my heart sank as I saw the familiar life of the city. My eyes were full of the evening sun, which I had not seen for some 180 hours. Passing through the streets, I looked around intently in search of a familiar face in the passing crowd.

I told the Germans that I was looking out for Ludwik. I swore at him in the worst possible way, saying he used to beat me at home, and I wanted revenge by finding him for them. These were Ludwik's instructions, of course.

I must have sounded convincing, for they asked me if I would like to work for them. I told them that this, of course, is my dream but not before I am a grown man, as I am still too young at present. The Germans were so sure of themselves, they seemed to swallow this outrageous lie.

We turned onto Jerusalem Avenue, and approached Kościuszko Parkway. The gathering dusk, and the serene Vistula, only heightened my turmoil. There are two roads leading to the gardens of the Lower Park. One of them ends by the shed, and the surrounding bushes give excellent cover for a vehicle of any kind. The other leads down the hill so that a car coming down is plainly visible. There is a small gate at the top where a car has to stop first. This helps to give adequate warning to anyone there to make a getaway. I took them this way, telling them it was a better road and would give them more chance to catch Ludwik if he happened to be in the gardens.

The plan was successful, for as we went down the hill I caught sight of two men running through the potato fields. The "POL" on the front of the car had been enough for them.

Quickly opening the small gate, we accelerated downhill and

159

screeched to a stop next to the shed. Two of the Gestapo men jumped out of the car with their machine guns pointed at some people gathered nearby, and after examining their identity cards, the Gestapo entered the shed.

After ten minutes of looking around they returned to the car with disappointed looks and shrugged, "*Nichts.*"

I was overjoyed, and had a hard time keeping my face from showing it.

Something must have inspired Ludwik to move our company's car.

While examining the identification papers of the people there, the Gestapo men noticed a young man of about twenty whose looks they did not like, and they took him with us in the car. He said he had arrived that morning on leave from labor in Germany. He had been looking for his uncle, but he was not at home, so he had come to the gardens. On the way back, he kept asking the Gestapo men for a cigarette. Poor fellow, he did not know the Gestapo yet. He said he had only five days' leave, and I knew the Germans would see to it that he spent them all in prison.

At nine o'clock in the evening, my "guardians" said good-bye to me at the Pawiak Prison gate, promising that I would be set free if I told the truth. My interrogation seemed to have ended for the day, since they did not take me back to Szucha Avenue.

So ended a day upon which my future—my life—depends.

FRIDAY, JULY 9

The days pass slowly, and my fantasies are getting worse. I have already seen too much in prison to believe that the Gestapo will set me free, and my imagination runs away with me in picturing what they will do to me instead.

SUNDAY, JULY 11

Today a long list of names was read of those who are to be transported to Auschwitz. Among them was mine.

I have given up all hope now as, according to rumors, we are to leave on Tuesday or Wednesday. Now I will find out for myself just what Uncle Norbert went through. Suddenly, I feel very cold. I don't want to die this way.

TUESDAY, JULY 13 MORNING

Tuesday morning, I was sitting in my cell in total despair, thinking about my parents whom I was now sure I would never see again. But the "*Kapo*," the criminal trustee, suddenly called to me, "You are being set free."

He gave me my release card. I just could not believe it!

But I was the only one who was silent. From the gloomy corners of the cell, sad jealous eyes looked at me and I heard everyone saying that I was lucky. The rule of Pawiak Prison is that the innocent go to Auschwitz, the guilty before a firing squad. Being released is almost unheard of.

Half an hour later I was sitting in the prison van on the way to Szucha Avenue.

Three pretty girls, their heads erect, were sitting by me in the van. Their quiet dignity caught my attention. I started to share my joy with them, but they told me that they were to be executed. The Germans had found out that they belonged to the Underground Army. They were Krystyna, sixteen years old; Barbara, seventeen years old; and Irena, twenty years old.

They told me about their fate so simply and openly that I did not know how to reply. Finally, I shook hands with each of them, and in this way paid tribute to their bravery. As a good-bye, they asked me to say a prayer for them in church.

Back at Szucha Avenue, I was put into the "sanitorium" waiting room again. A man sitting near me had a face which one could call neither human nor animal. His jaw and cheekbones were all out of place and covered with coagulated blood. In place of his right eye was a raw wound. I could only wonder how he was still alive.

A lady of about thirty years of age was sitting on the next chair, quietly discussing with a companion the tortures she had gone through. She was talking about them in a strangely matter-of-fact way, her arms crossed over bandages where her breasts used to be. She said she had been told that she would be put on the rack sometime the next day, and implied that she hoped everything would then end at last.

These people who, for their country or their faith, were suffering torture and death so bravely made a deep impression on me, and I could not help wondering if I would be so brave if it happened to me.

TUESDAY, JULY 13 AFTERNOON

This afternoon I was taken to the quarters of the officer in charge of Szucha Avenue.

I entered a large, coldly formal anteroom. On the wall was an enormous, full-length portrait of Hitler in dress uniform. The heavy, carved doors were flanked by long red and gold standards bearing the emblem of the twisted cross. As we came in, the guards opened these doors and there, behind an enormous desk, sat a huge man in a dark gleaming SS General's uniform, with silver trim and braided epaulettes. He looked so formidable that even the death's head insignia on his uniform seemed appropriate. With my shaven head, dirty clothes, and body shaking with hunger and fatigue, I had the sensation, not for the first time, of being less than human.

To my complete surprise, I noticed two other men at the desk —my father and Dr. Kipa, his translator. Seeing my father and not being able to greet him in the presence of the SS officer unnerved me; I noticed he was terribly pale and could barely stand. My imprisonment must have shaken him badly.

Some formalities and a lecture by the SS General followed. He told my father that he did not wish to set me free as he did not believe I was innocent, but that because of my age he was doing so this time. The next time, he threatened, nobody would be able to help me.

After that, in a dreamlike haze, I found myself at last on the way home, not able to believe I had really been set free from Pawiak Prison. I couldn't even talk to Father.

My underclothes were covered with the names and addresses of the families of my fellow prisoners. When I left, I had promised that I would contact these anxious people. It was one of the first things I did when I got home.

THURSDAY, JULY 15

My first day back on the streets of Warsaw. I felt I was being shadowed so I jumped from the moving streetcar. A man behind me left no doubt that I *was* being followed. I felt uneasy, angry. But, finally, I threw him off and got back home. As I entered the house, all was dark. Aunt Stacha, feeling her way past her wall of furniture, came creeping out of her room. "No more lightbulbs for Poles," she muttered, "just blackouts and curfews."

FRIDAY, JULY 16

I have told my father of yesterday's episode, and he has decided to send me to Baniocha at once. I took the narrow-gauge railway there this evening. Baniocha is another world, almost in another century, and all but untouched by the war. I found my mother in the secluded farmhouse which stands next to an apple orchard. The calm of the countryside seems as unreal to me as the time I have spent in prison.

SUNDAY, JULY 18

Mother is nervous. Mrs. Filipkiewicz was due here for lunch at 12:30 P.M.; it is now past three o'clock, and still she hasn't arrived from Warsaw. Mother tells me that Mrs. Filipkiewicz is going to help a local landowner sell some of his antiques, since he needs cash to keep his estate going.

MONDAY, JULY 19

Soon after 5:00 P.M. yesterday, an old countrywoman came rushing into the kitchen through the back door, sobbing loudly and crying, "They've killed Mrs. Filipkiewicz! They shot her right in front of my eyes!"

163

When Mother had calmed the old lady down a bit, she managed to tell us what had happened. Mrs. Filipkiewicz and she, along with several other women, had got a ride in a truck, on the road between Warsaw and Góra Kalwarja. A German patrol stopped the truck and asked the driver if he was transporting any Jews out of the city.

Without even being threatened, the miserable, cowardly wretch pointed to Mrs. Filipkiewicz and said, "There's one for you!"

The Germans immediately pulled Mrs. Filipkiewicz off the truck, and she showed them her false identity papers, swearing she was a practicing Catholic. The Germans seemed pretty convinced by this proud and dignified old lady, who spoke to them in their own language. But they whispered amongst themselves for a moment or two, then ordered Mrs. Filipkiewicz to kneel and say a Hail Mary. Since she remained silent, they shot her on the spot.

I could not believe my ears, for I couldn't comprehend how the driver could have done such a thing when he wasn't even under duress. Mother told me he must have been a *Volksdeutscher*. If he were Polish, he wouldn't have had a truck to drive and, in any case, would have been shot himself for helping a Jew to escape.

As a *Volksdeutscher*, he would receive money from the Germans for his actions, and that's probably why he picked up the poor lady in the first place.

Baniocha: The author (immediately following his release from Pawiak), Aunt Zosia, and Ludwik

WEDNESDAY, JULY 21

Ludwik surprised me by appearing at the gate of Baniocha this morning. He was preoccupied and worried, and all he wanted to talk about was Stefa. I gave him a detailed report of my imprisonment, and he said, "Well done." The closest he came to a smile was when I described my visit with the Gestapo to the Lower Park. He pressed me to give him all the details I could about Stefa, which I did, but said little in response.

MONDAY, JULY 26

Ludwik has left for Warsaw. I went with him to the station. He had an undefinably sad air about him. Nothing seems the same anymore.

SUNDAY, AUGUST 1

I am trying to forget everything by losing myself in the harvest celebrations of the countryside. With my young Aunt Zosia I went today to a nearby estate.

After an afternoon of dancing, we sat around a long table loaded with the traditional harvest thanksgiving meal. At the head of the table sat the owner of the estate, a handsome count in a green hunting jacket with a velvet collar. A middle-aged bachelor, his blue eyes twinkling in his lean weathered face, he graciously, but imperiously, scanned the loaded table and his dozens of guests. He was obviously proud that, even with a war on, he was able to maintain this ancient Slavic tradition of hospitality.

The Count had only to flick a finger and one of the serving girls would run to his side. He would whisper a few words and the girl would bustle off, with her long skirt and hair ribbons flapping as she ran.

The juicy hams, crisp brown ducks and geese, country bread and cheeses, were displayed on white linen decorated with golden oats, barley, and autumn vegetables. Large pitchers of milk and buttermilk were placed on the tables by buxom country girls. It was hard to believe that in Occupied Poland there were people indulg-

165

ing in such a feast. The Count must have been storing the food in secret for months.

I felt self-conscious. I was particularly ill at ease among the girls, with their long flowing tresses, and even the men, with their thick abundant hair. I felt naked and insignificant with my shaved skull. After Szucha Avenue, which, though unforgettable, now seemed an eternity away, I could only feel at home in the city. The scene around me appeared unreal. I felt as if I had been moved to another world. I tasted the food sparingly, but, although it was delicious, my body refused it.

Sitting next to me was a pretty young girl with huge dark eyes and soft brown hair. After dinner and dancing in the barn, I asked her to come for a walk with me. The sun was setting behind the harvested fields, and suddenly I felt alive again.

I told her how I felt—that it was not right to have such festivities when Warsaw was being terrorized by the Germans, when people there did not know where the next meal would come from and could not sleep for fear of the always-threatening knock of the Gestapo on their door.

During the walk, I learned that the girl came from Warsaw too. Her father had been arrested by the Germans some time ago, so she knew what I was talking about.

SUNDAY, AUGUST 8

Today, as every day, I went to the railway station to pick up the *New Warsaw Courier*. No news of what is really happening.

SATURDAY, AUGUST 14

I went again to the station in the afternoon to pick up the *New Warsaw Courier*. This issue is stamped across the front page with the words LONG LIVE THE POLISH ARMED FORCES. The Underground has been at work.

THURSDAY, AUGUST 26

The front page of today's paper carries sensational headlines: FIVE-MILLION ZŁOTY REWARD; ATTACK ON ARMED BANK TRANSPORT; THE WORK OF BANDITS. It is high time I got back to the city.

WEDNESDAY, SEPTEMBER 1

With the deepening of autumn I could not stay any longer. I said good-bye to Mother and took the train back to Warsaw.

SUNDAY, SEPTEMBER 5

I have been to see a friend, 'Dawid.' Together we have decided that, no matter the cost, we have to get more weapons. There is only one way—by disarming Germans.

WEDNESDAY, SEPTEMBER 15

Today we were able to borrow two guns from friends. 'Dawid' has a small automatic, a German-made Walther, while now I have in my possession a revolver, a very large caliber Smith & Wesson.

THURSDAY, SEPTEMBER 16

This morning we went by streetcar to Bielany, where the *Luftwaffe* airfield is situated. From there we went to a small wood concealing a path to a German military barrack. We crept about quietly and found a hiding place in the surrounding undergrowth.

We were unlucky. Although Germans passed by all the time, they always walked in twos and threes. A German on his own never came into view.

We waited over two and a half hours. At last, an old German on a bicycle came around the bend in the path. When we saw him, we jumped out from behind the bushes with our pistols and shouted, "Hands up!"

When he saw us and our guns he got down from his bicycle and raised his arms. I shoved my pistol into his chest while 'Dawid'

167

searched him. The German did not have any weapons. He saw that we were angry because he was unarmed, and begged us to take his bicycle and everything that he possessed, but to let him live.

'Dawid' jumped on the bicycle and made for home. I ordered the German to go down to the small ravine nearby, and told him that if he wished to live, he was to lie there for the next fifteen minutes.

When I was sure that he had no intention of moving, I ran as quickly as possible back to the station, and in ten minutes I was sitting in the streetcar on the way home.

FRIDAY, SEPTEMBER 17

'Dawid' and I went out again to look for armed Germans. I told my family I would not be back until very late.

It was getting late. Disappointed, angry, and ready for anything, we got into the German part of a streetcar, thinking that we might be lucky.

Near us there was a big German with the sign of the twisted cross on his lapel, and we decided to follow him from the streetcar. As he got out at the terminus on Słowacki Street, we noticed that he was carrying a large briefcase.

On one side of the street is the Fire Brigade Headquarters, and on the opposite side is a long wall surrounding the Opel assembly plant. In front of the plant are large gardens. It was ten o'clock and so dark that one could hardly see.

Leaving the streetcar stop, the German crossed the empty square in the direction of the Opel factory. We followed him, hugging the wall along the boulevard. He turned left and took Włościańska Street.

As he reached the corner, we approached him and shouted, "Hands up!" At the same time he felt the muzzle of my revolver against his head, and we dazzled him with the light of our flashlight. Frightened to death, he raised his arms.

Searching proved that this man was not carrying any arms. Furious, we began to swear. We took his briefcase and his wallet. The German, who could not understand what we were talking about, thought we were discussing how to kill him.

For want of anything better to do, we held the German for a few minutes and then ordered him to turn his back on us and run. He obviously thought we would shoot him while he was running and did not seem anxious to do what he was told, but when he saw just how determined we were, he obeyed. He did not stop until he had reached the gate of the factory.

We went down Słowacki Street toward Wilson Square, and on a dark side street we stopped to examine the contents of the brief-case and wallet. We learned that the German worked as a foreman of the Opel factory.

In the briefcase we found a few hard rolls with honey, which we ate ravenously. In the wallet, there were only some family snap-shots, a few *Deutsche marks*, and a ring.

By the time we reached Wilson Square the streets were deserted. We started to tear down signs pointing to German military installations located on the square. There were many signs since several major streets and roads pass through the square. We stacked all the signs together at one of the streetcar stops. There were more than twenty of them.

It was now long past midnight, and we waited to catch the last streetcar. When it arrived, I got into the driver's section; meanwhile, 'Dawid' loaded the signboards onto the rear platform of the tram. I then ordered the conductor to drive slowly along Mickiewicz Street in the direction of Inwalidów Square. As we moved along, 'Dawid' threw the signboards onto the pavement one after another, every few feet, and they broke into bits as they fell. We got off at Inwalidów Square and wandered around cautiously till daybreak.

SATURDAY, SEPTEMBER 18

Soon after dawn the curfew lifted, and we took the first streetcar into the city. It was empty. Over the Warsaw–Gdańsk viaduct, leading out of Żoliborz, we entered Bonifraterska Street, the boundary of the Ghetto ruins. As we passed the remains of the Wall on the right, I could see German SS policemen stationed there at intervals to guard the area. Beyond that I could see the fa-cades of the tall burned-out buildings still standing. In one of them I noticed, as I had done daily on my journeys into the city, a charred skeleton hanging in the window frame. In a strange way it comforted me, and I wanted it to remain. It proved to me somehow that the Ghetto was still there.

'Dawid' and I were now tired, hungry, and exasperated. We left the streetcar in the middle of Krasiński Square. As we walked around the square, the first signs of life were a couple of sanitation workers who were putting up a barricade around a manhole, in order to descend into the sewer. A German patrol walked past us with guns slung down toward the pavement. A few civilians began to enter the square on their way to work, and now and then a military truck lumbered by.

Suddenly, we noticed a tall German sergeant in full combat uniform, loaded with knapsacks, getting on a streetcar for Żoliborz. He must have been on his way to join his unit at the Russian Front. At his side hung a beautiful pistol, a German *Parabellum*, encased in a shining leather holster. Now that we had spotted such a weapon, it drew us like a magnet and we followed the sergeant onto the streetcar, going to the rear platform while he went to the front. The streetcar began to fill up. When we reached the Warsaw–Gdańsk Station stop, many people left the car and started to go down the curving concrete staircase leading to the station. One of them was the German sergeant, so we followed.

Looking around, we noticed three other German soldiers leaving the first car. They all had rifles, but did not seem to be in a hurry and were not paying any attention to us.

We ran quickly down the stairway and sheltered in the tunnel under the viaduct, ahead of the crowd. What we intended to do would take us only a few seconds, but every one of them counted. We knew we had to disarm the sergeant before the other three Germans descended the stairway. We barely had time enough to take our guns out of our pockets before the sergeant appeared, with a crowd of people behind him.

When he was about two meters from us we faced him and said, "Arms up quickly, or we will shoot."

He was obviously a seasoned combat soldier who would rather give up his life than his pistol. As he saw the muzzles of our guns pointing at him, he began to move slowly backward and instinctively started unfastening his holster.

170

Seeing this, we warned him once more, "Arms up, or you will die!" He ignored this. As we got closer to him, we could see his hand on his pistol and his finger on the safety catch.

There was no time to wait—it was either him or us. Quickly we raised our guns to eye level.

'Dawid' fired first.

We saw the German momentarily lift his arms in the air, and then he fell forward on his face. He died instantly.

The roar of the shot was still in our ears as the other three German soldiers ran out of the stairwell. There was no time to take the pistol from the body of the sergeant. We had to save ourselves. On one side were three soldiers and at the base of the viaduct were the German SS policeman, guarding the wall of the Ghetto.

Luckily for us, the frightened crowd began to run toward the station platform, and the Germans, thinking we were in the crowd, tried to stop everyone by firing.

In the meantime, we made a run for it along the base of the viaduct embankment. When we were halfway along the grassy slope we heard rifle bullets whiz past us. We turned and ran over the viaduct road and streetcar tracks, and down the opposite embankment. Then we crossed the open area on the street leading away from the Ghetto guards, and found refuge in the park behind Bonifraterska Street. From there, after catching our breath, we made our way to the Old City, and merged with the crowds on the Old Market Square.

Amazingly, we were safe. But to steady our nerves, we went into a small bar for a glass of vodka.

Then we returned home, by a circuitous and lengthy route to cover up our tracks.

On the way back, people told us we had better not go near the Warsaw–Gdańsk Station as the Gestapo and German SS police were around there stopping streetcars, searching and arresting all passersby.

MONDAY, SEPTEMBER 20

The SS police today brought a group of twenty perfectly innocent civilians into the gardens at the back of the viaduct embankment near the station, and there these poor souls were tied, gagged, and executed by a firing squad. Among the group were old people and children.

TUESDAY, SEPTEMBER 21

Military railway transports, loaded with tanks going to the Russian Front, have been dynamited near Warsaw.

WEDNESDAY, SEPTEMBER 22

I overheard my father saying to Mother that Leist had told him that the new head of the SS and Police for Warsaw is to be Franz Kutschera, "a man of wisdom and common sense."

MONDAY, SEPTEMBER 27

After the viaduct encounter and the German reprisals, rumors have made people around Żoliborz very aware of me again, so Father has sent me to the country once more in the hope that they'll forget about me.

FRIDAY, OCTOBER 22

I spent the early autumn with my mother at Baniocha. But after three weeks, I became very restless again and finally decided to return to Warsaw. However, because I was a marked man I could not engage in active Underground work, so I broke all my previous contacts with the exception of one—Ludwik.

MONDAY, OCTOBER 25

Kutschera has now replaced Stroop, just as Leist said.

WEDNESDAY, NOVEMBER 3

Late this afternoon, as darkness was already falling, I went to Ludwik's new apartment in Bielany; he is now living there under a new name.

He opened the door, and I could sense that he is a different man. For the first time I saw a bleak expression in his eyes. He had also changed physically—his thick hair is now clipped to a sharp stubble. I have always admired Ludwik for his energy, but now he seems to have lost all his initiative and optimism. He has never in the past been able to spare much time for me; now, with no one else around, he seems to have all the time in the world to spare. In one respect, though, he hasn't changed. In the past he has always dominated any conversations between us: he would do the talking and I would listen. Tonight was no different.

Lately, besides the leak that led to the arrest of Ola and so many others at the wedding, there have been a number of others from our battalion and other units close to the General Staff of the Home Army. Many more of Ludwik's friends have been lost, and the ruins of the Ghetto are still fresh in his mind.

From me and from others, Ludwik has learned that the Gestapo knows all about him. But he has no plans; his future seems to be a blank. Although we both know that he is a hunted man, Ludwik will not admit to himself, far less to me, that his role as company commander is compromised to such a point that it has crippled his Underground activities.

Any disguise for him is useless. He is so tall, so conspicuous, that he can never melt into a crowd. His only hope is to get out of Warsaw and join the Partisans, but this he will not do.

The little family circle that surrounded Ludwik has also gone; he cannot see Grandma and Marek; Stefa is in prison; and Ola is dead. Stefa's arrest has hit him especially hard. He describes, almost incoherently, a plan he has for freeing Stefa before the train takes her to Auschwitz.

Losing Stefa is the quintessence of everything else Ludwik has lost. But, more than anything else, it is inaction that is driving him to desperation. In Pawiak Prison, and after the viaduct encounter, I lost my real fear of death. Now I know that I have to devote my

PAWIAK WILL BE AVENGED

time to avenging, no matter how, the wrongs done to my country, my family, and my friends. But Ludwik's dream is still to lead his company into action, and fate, it seems, is denying him that chance.

I tell Ludwik that I, too, want to get back into action. But because of my arrest and what happened later at the viaduct I cannot now be a part of 'Baszta.' So, I want to join the Commandos or the Partisans. Many of Ludwik's other recruits, and even officers from 'Baszta,' are already doing this. This adds to Ludwik's hurt.

It depresses me utterly to see him this way, but I am powerless to help him.

SUNDAY, NOVEMBER 21

I keep trying in every possible way to join the Commandos and get back into active duty. That way, I would have many chances to fight.

But after the heightened terror in the summer of 1943 they have stopped recruiting. Still, I am not totally idle, and for the time being I have taken over a signal company section.

TUESDAY, NOVEMBER 23

I was busy training six soldiers belonging to my section today, when I got the news.

Someone came and told me that, a few blocks away, on Śmiała Street, a man called Ludwik Berger had been shot. When I heard this, I ran out of the house and raced like a fool to the spot where the incident was supposed to have taken place.

I searched about and to my horror, at the foot of the chain-link fence which separated two gardens, I saw bits of flesh, coagulated blood, and pieces of bone on the ground.

Ludwik Berger—'Goliat'—'Michał'—'Hardy'—my leader, was dead! I would not, could not, believe it. But, the dark stain near my feet spoke for everything—for the cruel and bitter truth.

Standing to attention, I said the words of a prayer and took an oath of revenge on those who had murdered my commander.

I seemed unable to move from the spot, standing there in silence and deep thought for a long time.

At last, I went to the nearest house, where I knocked and asked for information about the incident. I heard that a few hours earlier, the Germans had carried out a street search. This time, it was the streetcar stops on Mickiewicz Street at the intersections with Zajączek Street and Inwalidów Square that were simultaneously surrounded by large numbers of SS police. They halted all streetcars, ordered the passengers out, and began checking. Unfortunately, Ludwik, with a friend, was in one of the cars.

When the two men saw the German SS surrounding the approaching streetcar stop, they jumped out and started to run across the square and down Polish Army Avenue toward Śmiała Street. Spotting the escaping men, the Germans opened fire with their machine guns and wounded Ludwik in the arm.

But the two men had already entered Śmiała Street and were running toward Zajączek Street. When they saw German SS men at this intersection, Ludwik and his companion turned and ran into the garden of the nearest house.

Ludwik—his arm bleeding badly—knocked at the door of the house to ask for shelter. But the Germans were already close behind him, so Ludwik turned away and tried to escape across the neighboring gardens. His friend, 'Lenin,' ran in the opposite direction and escaped, but Ludwik was spotted by a young SS man, who ran after him and opened fire with his machine gun.

This race for life and death continued across the small gardens. Though wounded, Ludwik moved swiftly, and the German's bullets missed their target.

Ludwik then found himself at the wire fence. The German had used up all his ammunition. If only Ludwik had succeeded in getting over the fence, he might have made it to safety. But his enemy, seeing Ludwik starting to climb over it, threw his gun down and attacked him with his bare hands.

Both of them were tall and well built, but Ludwik was weak from loss of blood and could only use one of his hands—his wounded arm prevented him from using the other.

After a few minutes' struggle, Ludwik had the German on the

176

ground under him and, with one hand holding him down, he sank his teeth into his enemy's throat. It was his only way of fighting when he had no weapon.

But another German shot Ludwik in the head, blowing out his brain.

TUESDAY, NOVEMBER 30

I feel the need of revenge but can do little without revealing my connection with Ludwik. So I went out today with my friend Marek and we tore down the street signs at all corners of Czarniecki Street. Stacking them together, we then carried the load to his house.

SATURDAY, DECEMBER 4

The two of us have been working on the street signs, and this evening after dark we took them back; then, with the assistance of another friend, we rehung them. This time the signs read: MICHAŁ-HARDY STREET. It is the least I can do.

WEDNESDAY, DECEMBER 8

The Germans have removed our street signs.

THURSDAY, DECEMBER 16

Now more restless than ever, I have been increasing my efforts to get into the Commandos, and today I finally succeeded. I have joined the Commando Company of Żoliborz. My friend 'Wilk' made it possible. He already belongs to the Ninth Commando Company, and is the leader of one of its sections, to which I am assigned.

In my search to join the Commandos and to fight, I have found the right group. When 'Wilk' heard my stories of Pawiak Prison and Szucha Avenue, of Ludwik and Ola, and of the Ghetto, he decided that I had won the right to a place in their ranks.

FRIDAY, DECEMBER 24

I attended the first meeting today and got to know some of the others belonging to our section. They are 'Sławek,' 'Bogdan,' and 'Kacper.'

I have taken Ludwik's original pseudonym, 'Goliat.'

1944

SUNDAY, JANUARY 2

A Commando attack was mounted early this morning against a group of Germans returning to Warsaw from a hunting expedition. Fischer was known to be in the party, and the machine-gun fire was concentrated on his car. News of this attack reached Warsaw very quickly, but no details were given as to its success or otherwise.

This evening when Father came home, I heard him telling Mother that Leist had taken him into the City Hall courtyard this morning and had pointed to his bullet-ridden limousine. Leist was extremely agitated at coming so close to death, and had asked Father to contact the Underground, reminding them of Leist's humanitarian attitude toward the population. Father says he told Leist that he would like to do as requested, but that he had no contact with any "Underground."

MONDAY, JANUARY 3

Confirmation came through today that the attack had indeed been aimed at Fischer and not at Leist. There had been a last-minute switch of cars by the Germans, however, and that was how Leist's car came to be fired upon by mistake.

TUESDAY, FEBRUARY 1

Another Commando attack was made today, in which 'Lot' threw a bomb at Kutschera's car; Kutschera was killed. This action was a reprisal for the now almost daily mass executions of innocent people on the streets of Warsaw. So much for the "common sense policy" which Leist had said Kutschera would bring to Warsaw! Unfortunately, 'Lot' himself was badly wounded in the attack, and he died soon afterward in the hospital where Aunt Zosia works. Another from our battalion is gone.

THURSDAY, FEBRUARY 3

A notice was posted on Wilson Square this morning. In retribution for Kutschera's death, the Germans are levying another fine on the

181

city—this time, they want 100 million *złoty*. Nobody needed telling what would happen if the fine weren't paid on time.

FRIDAY, FEBRUARY 4

Whole sections of the city were cleared today in preparation for Kutschera's funeral; it reminds us of Hitler's victory parade in October 1939, when they also cleared people away from the parade route. The Germans are sparing no effort to give Kutschera a fitting funeral, but they are also taking no chances by giving Warsaw's population a good opportunity to fire at them—they are still as nervous and afraid as they were back in 1939!

FRIDAY, FEBRUARY 11

On my way to Leszno Church today, I saw a crowd of people standing in front of the Wall. They were gazing at something above the Wall, on the Ghetto side of it. As I got closer, I could see for myself —hung from the upper-story balconies of what had been an apartment house were the bodies of twenty-two of our Freedom Fighters.

I was horrified, and cold with anger, yet at the same time amazed that the Germans couldn't see that such actions only encouraged us to fight back even harder than before.

MONDAY, FEBRUARY 21

'Kacper,' a member of our Commando company, went with a friend to disarm Germans in the vicinity of Napoleon Square this morning, and while doing so his pistol refused to fire. He had failed to check it. A German military car passing by saw him with the gun in his hand. The car stopped, and in a few minutes the unfortunate 'Kacper' found himself with his captors on the way to Szucha Avenue. We have received no news from him since.

Leszno Street hanging

THURSDAY, FEBRUARY 24

With 'Kacper' gone, only six of us are left with 'Wilk.' He is a determined, no-nonsense Commando, and his pseudonym (meaning Wolf) suits him well. He is a serious young man, honest and brave, and a natural leader. The men believe in 'Wilk'; they trust him implicitly and would follow him anywhere. He never fails their trust.

'Wilk' is only two years older than myself, and he, too, has had to lie about his age in order to join the Commandos and to be a candidate for the officer training school. Prior to joining our company, 'Bogdan,' 'Sławek,' and he were members of the *Szare Szeregi* (Gray Rows), made up of prewar Boy Scouts. While I spent my early Underground career in the Home Army's 'Baszta' Battalion, they spent theirs in the Gray Rows, in small sabotage and intelligence work.

MONDAY, FEBRUARY 28

I am disturbed by the news that came through today. Our detachment has been taken over by a new leader, 'Korwin,' as 'Wilk' has left for the Cadet-Officers' School.

183

'Korwin' does not seem to like me, and he takes it out on me whenever he can. It is unpleasant, but as his subordinate, there is not much I can do about it.

There is a certain air of indecisiveness about 'Korwin,' and he seems arbitrary in his acts. He has the rather unfortunate need to make himself look better by running others down. At the same time, he is an extrovert, very creative and full of imagination, and has a keen sense of humor.

FRIDAY, MARCH 3

I turned fifteen today, so it has become that much more vital for me to obtain the best possible legal cover if I am to continue my Underground work and not be subject to forced labor or be deported to Germany. I have thought hard. What I need is a job that will take a minimum of time and will allow me to move freely on the streets of the city.

I know the Germans respect external signs of officialdom and legality, stamps, documents, signatures, and above all, uniforms. But there are few uniforms that command respect which a Pole can wear now. The "Blue" Police uniform is no longer a badge of honor; many of its present members are weak and corrupt, and they have degraded the prewar Polish Police.

I can think of only one which commands the respect of Poles and Germans alike, because it signifies safety for both. That is the fireman's uniform. The city's fire departments, which performed so gallantly during the 1939 Battle of Warsaw, have maintained their professional integrity throughout the Occupation. I meet all the physical requirements of a volunteer fireman recruit, so I have decided to try to join the Fire Brigade as soon as I possibly can.

WEDNESDAY, MARCH 8

The air-raid alarms in Warsaw have resumed. Bombers of the Soviet Air Force have begun night raids on Poland. At night the city is shrouded in total blackness, and the penalties for not observing Civil Defense precautions are severe. There is suddenly a shortage of trained and experienced firemen. Additional responsibilities, consisting mainly of jobs previously assigned to Civil Defense authorities, are being put upon Warsaw's fire departments. This will help me in joining the Fire Brigade.

MONDAY, MARCH 20

I was accepted as a fireman today. There are now four of us in the Ninth Company Commandos who wear this uniform—'Bratek,' 'Rudy,' 'Biczan,' and myself.

Author, age fifteen, wearing uniform of Fire Brigade Cadet-Officer, 1944

We will all make full use of the uniform in carrying out our Underground work, of course, particularly at night. As firemen, we are allowed to be on the streets after curfew hour while on duty—going back and forth to the station, to fires, and to observation posts. Even if stopped by German patrols—which hardly ever happens—one is usually allowed to carry on with only a slight delay. Having a uniform and fire-fighting equipment is a great help in our resistance activities, and we are able to perform a useful and worthwhile job as well.

SATURDAY, APRIL 1

I have been assigned to the Żoliborz Fire Station in my home neighborhood. It is a large, modern building with the latest fire-fighting equipment. Our hook-and-ladder truck is new and beautifully maintained, as are all the other trucks and equipment at our disposal. On the first floor are the garages, offices, and training facilities. The upper floors consist mainly of large modern dormitories. Apart from the stairs, the main link that connects virtually all the floors is a traditional fireman's pole.

Among the first training exercises is the use of this pole. Before the final ring of the alarm bell dies down we have to jump out of bed, don our equipment, and quickly slide down to the garage where the trucks are waiting with their engines already turned on. It is a test of skill. So are the other training exercises we go through: the drills, use of the high ladder while wearing our full equipment and wielding the heavy fire hose, fire-fighting, and rescue methods. Teamwork is called for as much as skill and concentration are needed, and we certainly need to be in good physical shape, which is difficult on our meager rations.

SUNDAY, APRIL 2

Since I live near Polish Army Avenue, I have been given duty at an observation post there. My teammate is 'Bratek,' an intelligent and friendly young man, only about two or three years older than myself. He has a quick mind and a great sense of humor, and I thoroughly enjoy the discussions we have during our long night vigils. He and I get along very well together, and he shares my enthusiasm for the dual nature of our work.

SATURDAY, APRIL 15

Tonight again, after the wailing sirens stopped, we could hear the distant drone of the approaching Soviet bombers. Then the criss-cross movements of the powerful antiaircraft searchlights began, as they rhythmically swept across and probed the night skies. We could see the silhouetted shapes of the aircraft as they struggled to evade the bright beams and sought refuge in darkness beyond. The climax was noisy and fearful, as the bombs and incendiaries fell on the city, which was illuminated by the flames of the fires that followed.

TUESDAY, APRIL 25

'Bratek' and I have become really good friends. We talk about our work in the Commandos and our common dream—an open fight against the Germans. We know what we face and what we have to do, and we don't like having to wait for the right time to get started.

WEDNESDAY, MAY 3

It is the Third of May, Poland's national holiday. We are now in the fifth year of the Occupation, and everyone longs with increasing impatience for freedom. I guess everyone refuses to consider the possibility that we will *not* regain our freedom.

The Germans have marked the day by placing three times as many police patrols as usual on the streets, filling the city streets with open trucks loaded with SS police, and installing machine-gun emplacements in front of every German military building. The Germans are more jittery now because of the huge Russian offensive opening up on the Eastern Front.

Even on this special day the Germans will not permit people to attend the May Mass in church after curfew in the evening. This service is held throughout the month in honor of the Virgin Mary, but has to take place *before* the curfew hour. Moreover, both the singing of patriotic hymns in church and the preaching of sermons making reference to politics are strictly forbidden.

This afternoon I decided to attend the service. Saint Stanisław Kostka Church in Żoliborz was crowded. Shafts of mellow sunlight fell from its tall, narrow windows onto the people below. The sheltered archways were banked with red and white flowers, and soft candlelight cast flickering shadows on the white walls.

I went straight up to the top gallery, which was also full, and stood by the door leading to the organ loft. I had decided that it

Saint Stanisław Kostka Church, Żoliborz

would be grand if one of the oldest Polish melodies could be played during the holiday service. So, near the end of the service I knocked on the door, and after a while the violinist opened it and asked what I wanted. I showed him that I had a pistol under my jacket. The pistol was not loaded, of course, and I wouldn't have used it here anyway, but I hoped *he* wouldn't know this.

I was let in at once. The door was closed behind me, and I approached the organist who was just ending one of the melodies specially intended for the May service. While the organ sheltered me from the sight of the congregation, I again showed my pistol and asked the organist in honor of our great day to play the hymn "God, Who Hath Poland Saved," which had been our national hymn since the Uprising of 1830.

Neither my pistol nor my words would persuade the organist. He said he could not do it, for if he did, the priest and he and all his family would be executed. While talking to me he did not stop playing.

I explained to the organist that he would have witnesses—the violinist and the vocalist—to the fact that he had had to play the hymn at gunpoint. To my delight, when he had finished the one he was playing, he struck the chords of our national hymn, and to everyone's surprise and joy we heard the stanzas of the melody that touches the heart of every Pole. They were all so taken aback that nobody even moved. The people in the gallery were the first to begin singing, and they were soon followed by everyone else. The whole church then reverberated with the melody and words of the hymn:

> God, who held Poland for so many ages,
> In Your protection, glory, and great power;
> Who gave Your wisdom to her bards and sages,
> And gave Your own shield as her rightful dower.
> Before Your altars, we in supplication
> Kneeling, implore You, free our land and nation.
> Bring back to Poland ancient mights and splendor,
> And fruitful blessings bring to fields and meadows;
> Be once again our Father, just, tender,
> Deliver us from our dire shadows.

As the chorus repeated the refrain, the church was filled with the heartrending phrase:

> Before Your altars, we in supplication
> Kneeling, implore You, free our land and nation.

I did not wait any longer. I vanished from the church into the twilight, the last emotional words of the hymm resounding in my ears.

The people realized, of course, what might happen to them. In five minutes not a living soul remained in the church.

THURSDAY, MAY 4

The news of yesterday's church service has spread throughout Żoliborz and cheered the people up. I ran into the organist on the street today, and he politely bowed and smiled at me.

MONDAY, MAY 15

We learned today of the successful attack by our Commandos on the airfield at Bielany, in which many planes were destroyed. We were also informed that our Commando group will soon begin nighttime field maneuvers in order to test our weapons and training under simulated combat conditions. We have received quite thorough training in handling weapons and in the theoretical part of military preparation—but only to the extent that it is possible to get this from army training manuals, which have been read and studied in small groups in private homes.

What we need is to train as a full combat team in practical field exercises. So, our company—now about 130 strong—is planning to meet soon for nighttime exercises.

THURSDAY, JUNE 1

We made our way stealthily to Żoliborz Lower Park this evening. After short training exercises there, the company moved to another place for firing exercises. We carefully marched through the streets of Żoliborz, past the guards of the Opel factory, to the housing colony of Słodowiec. There we left the railroad tracks, which we had been following, and approached the open sand dunes of the prewar army training grounds.

As I was pulling my Sten gun out from under my coat, the extra magazine fell into the sand. Then I heard a booming voice behind me, "Pick it up with your teeth!" I hesitated for a split second, and I heard a second order, "Pick it up now!" It was that bastard, 'Korwin.' Trust him to be around at the wrong moment!

Still holding the Sten gun in my right hand, I bent down and grabbed the long metal magazine with my teeth. I straightened up with my mouth full of gritty white sand, to find 'Korwin's' towering figure before me.

"Keep the damned thing in your mouth," he said as he noticed my attempt to remove it in order to spit out the sand. "That bush over there—get down and crawl there and back ten times. That ought to teach you how to take care of your weapon!"

After I had crawled back and forth in the sand like a land crab, hating being reprimanded so publicly, I got up, spat out a mouthful of sand, and joined the detachment on the firing line. I vowed I would never again drop a weapon.

We were now on the ground in our firing positions, waiting for dawn so that we could start shooting, only too well aware that there were numerous and well-armed German units in the immediate vicinity.

Then, slowly, the morning sun's rays fell upon the distant bull's-eye targets on the concrete bunkers. The first to fire were those with short arms, then those with rifles, and finally those with Sten guns. I fired a short burst, quickly reloaded the magazine, fired another short burst, and waited. A long burst from Lieutenant 'Szymura's' machine gun followed. The sun's low rays cast deep shadows on the sand dunes in front of us, and an eerie silence reigned as the last bullets from the machine gun splattered off the concrete bunkers.

And then, over the horizon, a large platoon of *Wehrmacht* soldiers emerged from the direction of Lower Marymont in full combat formation. They soon took up positions and started firing. The order came down our line to lie still and not to return their fire.

Then 'Korwin' repeated 'Szymura's' statement that the Germans were shooting with blanks. This gave us much-needed assurance. It was only a group of German soldiers out on early morning firing practice, just like ourselves. We gathered up our weapons, hid them under our long jackets, and dispersed in small groups.

WEDNESDAY, JUNE 7

The news of the Allied invasion of Europe yesterday has spread through the city like wildfire. It is the only topic of discussion in the house today.

Father says this could well be a major turning point in the war —maybe even the "beginning of the end," to paraphrase Churchill's words—and he also says many people in City Hall are convinced that liberation is just around the corner now.

He himself is more cautious, as he knows the German reaction will probably be the declaration of a state of full emergency. In fact, he is convinced that things will still get worse, reminding us of the Germans' original statement that if they ever have to leave Poland, they will first make sure they leave no one alive here.

THURSDAY, JUNE 8

Today my company engaged in street action against a *Volksdeutscher* collaborator—Bolongino—carrying out another sentence passed by the Underground Court on a war criminal. My friend 'Gozdawa' was killed in the action.

SATURDAY, JULY 1

Poland is now under the shadow of the Red Army too. Day and night the ground trembles with the roar of the guns, always coming nearer. At night the Red Air Force mounts raids on the city. Long transports of evacuated Germans, officers and men, come and go through Warsaw.

The Red Army reentered Poland early this year. With diplomatic relations between Moscow and the Polish Government-in-Exile broken, we heard Prime Minister Mikołajczyk broadcasting on the radio from England that we would have preferred to meet the Soviet Army as allies.

MONDAY, JULY 10

We have heard that the leaders of the Communist Underground have been in Moscow since March and that Stalin is going to make them the future Government of Poland. He has promised to supply the People's Army (AL) with weapons for the Uprising. The main thorn in his side in our Home Army.

WEDNESDAY, JULY 12

General Bór-Komorowski has issued an order to all Home Army commanders, telling them that the Russians do not recognize the legal Government of Poland and are trying to overthrow it:

> We must be prepared for an open collision between Poland and the Soviets, and for our part we must fully demonstrate in such a collision the independent position of Poland.

We hear that the Communists want to incorporate our Home Army units into their puppet Polish People's Army. For this reason, our leaders have called off the nationwide Uprising set for this month.

MONDAY, JULY 17

We have recently been receiving a lot of weapons from RAF airdrops. But now, with the short summer nights, the drops will be coming to an end just when we need them the most. However, quite a few weapons are coming from home production. Still, there is an inadequate supply of ammunition.

Our company has received a number of weapons from the airdrops. Among them are a few British-made PIAT antitank bazookas, which came packed in their original containers; these are very bulky, and we were at a loss as to how to dispose of them.

'Korwin' has finally solved our problem. Today he pedaled his rickshaw downtown and hired a couple of men with a horse and wagon, without, of course, telling them what they were to transport. When they found out what they were loading onto their wagon, they became afraid, but they did not refuse to cooperate. 'Korwin' jotted down their names and addresses, just as a precaution, and drove with them to the edge of the Great Kampinoska Forest, where they hid the containers. He said that upon returning to town the two men, being loyal Poles, refused money for their services. But they did agree to have a couple of drinks on 'Korwin.'

WEDNESDAY, JULY 19

We have received some brand-new Colt .45s and I have been given the responsibility of storing five of them. I decided to hide them under the roof insulation in the attic at home.

As luck would have it, however, Father came home this afternoon and told me he expected that the house would soon be searched again by the Gestapo. He asked me if I had any incriminating material at home. I hesitated, because the security of the guns was foremost in my mind, but then decided I owed it to the family to tell the truth. When I told him what I had hidden in the attic, Father suggested we immediately move the guns to the house of a trusted friend of his near the Lower Park. He then put the pistols in a briefcase and we took them off to a new hiding place. I immediately reported the new place of the arms cache to my commander, telling him why I had revealed the location of the pistols. He said he understood my predicament.

THURSDAY, JULY 20

I have been afraid that the Germans would succeed in leaving Poland without being punished and without a fight—unpunished for Ludwik, Ola, and Zula, for Uncle Norbert, and for hundreds of thousands of others. After years of training and waiting for the chance of an open fight; after the Ghetto; after the street hunts and public executions; after the gas chambers, and the years of humiliating Occupation, all of us are eagerly awaiting the final fight.

Now it is coming! The liberation of Warsaw is coming!

Our company has finished its training and is not allowed to leave the city, so today I decided to go over to Mickiewicz Street to see my girl friend, Marysia. She lives in an apartment building there known as the Glass House. It was a hot, sticky summer day, and Żoliborz, usually so green, was covered in dust. I reached the Glass House just before noon and knocked on Marysia's apartment door. She opened it quickly and let me in. Her mother was there, and Marysia was upset about something, so we went up on the roof for some air.

I put my arm around her and tried to console her. After a while she calmed down, and we walked around the huge roof which commands a spectacular view of Żoliborz.

As we walked at the edge of the roof terrace above Mickiewicz Street, I saw an abandoned tank to one side. I asked Marysia whether she knew what it was doing there—this was the first time I had seen a tank on the streets of Warsaw since the Battle of the Ghetto in 1943.

She said it was broken down but, of course, everybody is afraid to investigate it. Just last month they shot a small boy for touching a motorcycle.

Marysia and I then went for a walk through Żeromski Park, and afterwards up to the top of the viaduct over the Warsaw–Gdańsk Station. There was very little activity except for a long line of slowly moving horse-drawn carts and tired, dusty Hungarian Army troops withdrawing from the Front. The mangy old horses could hardly pull their sorry loads up the viaduct. A few Hungarians walked alongside the carts, with machine pistols sloppily suspended from their shoulders. Each gave us a pitiful but friendly smile and a wave of the hand. I returned the greeting, jealously eyeing the beautiful German arms going to such complete waste. I whispered into Marysia's ear, "I wish I had a pint of vodka on me. I heard recently that you can now easily get pistols from these guys in return for our vodka."

When we returned to the Glass House, the apartment was empty. We ate some sandwiches and had some hot tea, not saying much but enjoying our snack. Then I heard a knock at the door. It was a messenger with instructions from 'Wilk.'

I got back to our headquarters as quickly as I could. 'Wilk' told me that a state of emergency now exists and that, because of the lack of accommodations, all the group will have to stay at my home on Feliński Street.

Our detachment has settled in, taking over the whole house—except for my Aunts' quarters, of course! We are not allowed to leave the house at all, even to go into the garden. My bedroom has become our headquarters, and we are spending our time making plans. We are also spending an inordinate amount of time cleaning our few handguns.

FRIDAY, JULY 21

We hear there has been an attempt on Hitler's life! 'Wilk' thinks they have killed the son of a bitch and that we should start the Uprising immediately, otherwise we will not have a chance to fight. He believes that, once we start fighting, the British and Polish air units will drop paratroopers and that together we will liberate Warsaw before the Russians get here.

SUNDAY, JULY 23

Our entire Ninth Commando Company has been put on active alert. All the detachments are now located in Żoliborz, except the Fifth Detachment from the 230th Platoon. That detachment, consisting of men living across the river in the Praga section of Warsaw, is placed on alert there.

MONDAY, JULY 24

Time drags as we wait nervously for the great moment when we will engage in an open fight with our enemy.

My home is the center for the distribution of soup to some fifty men of our platoon, all staying at different houses in Żoliborz. Our company, as the only Commando company in Żoliborz, is of course going to fight in this part of Warsaw. I am happy to be defending and freeing my own home and neighborhood.

TUESDAY, JULY 25

All detachements are busy. Some are engaged in gathering a strange assortment of uniforms—helmets borrowed from the crosses over the graves of Polish soldiers who fell in the 1939 defense of the city, or combat camouflage jackets of the SS *Panzer* units taken from a nearby factory. The girls of our company are making red and white armbands—the only standard part of our otherwise crazy mixture of civilian and military outfits of all ages, styles, and colors.

'Wilk' is the only one dressed in a regular army uniform. Where he found it, I do not know. In his green gray outfit, army boots, field cap with a large white eagle and Cadet-Officer's stripe, he cuts an imposing figure. His Sten gun, suspended on a leather strap from his shoulder, completes the picture. His neat appearance contrasts sharply with that of most of the group.

We hear that fresh armored battalions of the enemy are passing through on their way to the Front. They must be quite a contrast to the tired and dirty German troops we saw retreating from the Front a few days ago.

WEDNESDAY, JULY 26

We were fiddling with the radio set today when we came across the faint and broken sentences of Radio Moscow broadcasting in Polish:

> Warsaw . . . hears . . . the . . . guns . . . Polish Army . . . trained in the USSR, is now joined by the People's Army to form . . . the Polish Armed Forces. . . . Its ranks will be joined tomorrow by the sons of Warsaw. They . . . wipe out the Hitlerian vermin. . . . Poles, the time of liberation is at hand! Poles, to arms!

We have been sitting here for almost a week, and now the Communists are going to beat us to the fight!

THURSDAY, JULY 27

At five o'clock this evening the loudspeakers blared out a new proclamation by Fischer. Tomorrow, all men between the ages of seventeen and sixty-five must report for trench-digging and other work connected with the fortification of the city. A minimum of 100,000 men must report promptly at 8:00 A.M.

Father is shaken by this news. It could as easily mean deportation, the gas chambers, or execution squads for all able-bodied men, as providing cannon fodder for the Soviet artillery. The men of our detachment take it as a possible leak of our contemplated

Uprising and a German effort to suppress it. In any case, we feel that it will only speed up "W-Hour."

FRIDAY, JULY 28

In the morning, Aunt Stacha went to see how the mobilization of men for the "trench work" was proceeding. She arrived at one of the posts shortly after 8:00 A.M., and all she saw was a handful of men assembled, mostly elderly and invalids. At 9:00 A.M. the military trucks left empty.

SATURDAY, JULY 29

During the night, there was heavy Soviet mass bombing of the city. We hear Soviet tanks have reached Praga.

SUNDAY, JULY 30

Long lines of heavy tanks from the SS Hermann Göring *Panzer* Division passed along Jerusalem Avenue today on the way to Praga; we heard later that the Red Army is withdrawing under the onslaught of the German reinforcements.

MONDAY, JULY 31

"W-Hour" has been set for tomorrow at 17:00 hours. Our time has come!

TUESDAY, AUGUST 1

It was a parched summer morning. At dawn we got orders to move into a house at Tucholska Street, off Krasiński Street, where our whole platoon had gathered. Here, additional arms were distributed among us.

TUESDAY, AUGUST 1   MIDDAY

Along with a few others I was chosen to go on patrol to Suzina Street, our pistols and Sten guns hidden under our jackets. We were to protect another detachment of our company, which was engaged in moving arms from one of our hideouts. Our orders were not to shoot unless first fired upon.

When we got to the corner of Krasiński and Suzina Streets, we divided into pairs at the intersection and waited, more alert than ever before to everything that was happening around us.

We did not have to wait long.

From Kochowska Street the advance group, led by 'Świda,' carrying two large packages, entered Krasiński Street, while 'Korwin' and 'Longinus' ran into 'Wilk' and 'Horodeński' going toward Suzina Street.

At that moment, a German patrol truck drove quite slowly down Krasiński Street. Seeing the column, the Germans brought the vehicle to a screeching halt and opened fire on the men in the middle of the boulevard.

A boulevard of war, Krasiński Street, Żoliborz

199

'Świda' responded with his Sten gun; one of his men pulled a light machine gun out of a sack, took up position and, after firing a short salvo, uttered a curse: his gun was stuck. At that moment, 'Wilk' and 'Horodeński' entered the action.

The Germans, surprised by the fire on their flank from the other side of Krasiński Street, turned around. This gave the opportunity to the 'Świda' group to withdraw to Kochowska Street.

The firing was still fierce, and bullets whined over our heads as we lay flat in the green center strip dividing the boulevard. I kept firing back, 'Wilk' wounded a couple more of them with his Sten gun, and the Germans withdrew quickly toward Powązki. During this exchange of fire, 'Horodeński' was wounded, and he and 'Wilk' withdrew to the Lower Park.

Having a few minutes' respite, we unpacked the arms and distributed the guns, hand grenades, and ammunition among us. I drew an old Polish army rifle—the *Warszawiak* 1937—with ammunition. Then we took up positions in the buildings along Krasiński Street.

TUESDAY, AUGUST 1 AFTERNOON

It was then early afternoon. Two huge German trucks, loaded with special SS anti-insurgency Commandos, stopped on the boulevard and began firing into Suzina Street with machine guns and rifles. We in turn opened up on them, and their bullets roared over our heads and hit the walls of the apartment building from which we were firing. This exchange of fire gave me my first opportunity to use my newly acquired rifle. At one point, we had had no wounded, although several Germans had been struck by our bullets. Then, however, after half an hour's engagement, I saw that two of our men had been hit and were being carried to a nearby house. The Germans, who had not yet been really able to reach us with their fire, sent a sharpshooter to the end of the street opposite us in order to gauge our exact location. One had to admit that he showed great bravery, for his mission pretty well marked him for certain death.

To our amazement, without any cover, the sharpshooter crossed the whole distance between the place where the German trucks were situated and the end of our street. Only there, when

The beginning of the 1944 Uprising

he was facing us, did a bullet from Cadet-Officer 'Mirski's' gun strike him.

The Germans withdrew with their trucks, and we are going to move to a house on Mierosławski Street where we intend to stay until it is time to rejoin our company.

TUESDAY, AUGUST 1 EVENING

At exactly five o'clock, as planned, a wave of explosions and bursts of automatic rifle fire set off the Uprising throughout the city. In the midst of the dust and fire, white and red flags (not seen since 1939) were raised along the streets and fluttered from windows and rooftops to hail this great moment.

German tanks were on the corners of all the main boulevards and squares, and their shells and machine-gun fire prevented our units from crossing the streets. Heavy gunfire, machine guns, and

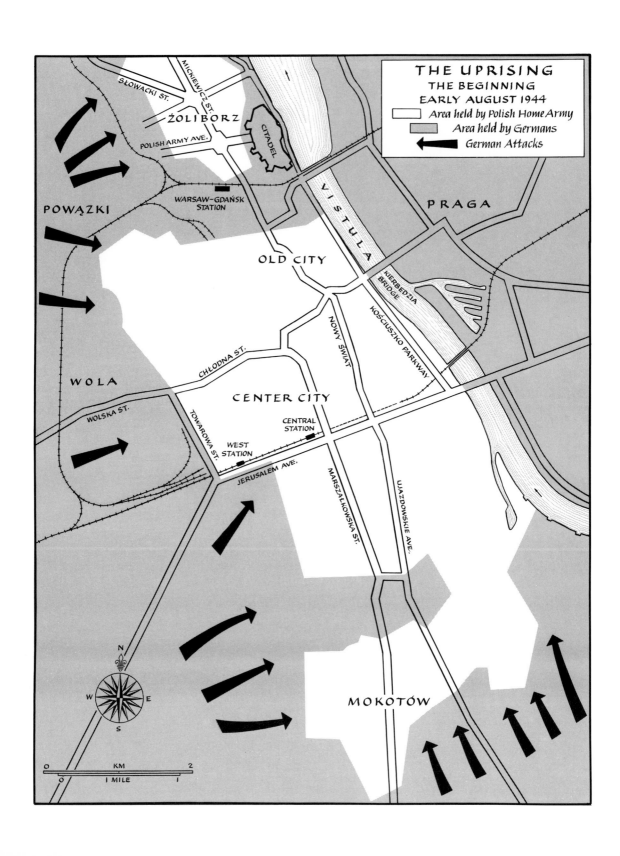

THE UPRISING
THE BEGINNING
EARLY AUGUST 1944

Area held by Polish Home Army
Area held by Germans
German Attacks

SŁOWACKI ST.
MICKIEWICZ ST.
ŻOLIBORZ
CITADEL
POLISH ARMY AVE.
WARSAW–GDAŃSK STATION
POWĄZKI
PRAGA
VISTULA
OLD CITY
KIERBEDZIA BRIDGE
NOWY ŚWIAT
KOSCIUSZKO PARKWAY
CHŁODNA ST.
WOLA
CENTER CITY
WOLSKA ST.
TOWAROWA ST.
CENTRAL STATION
WEST STATION
JERUSALEM AVE.
MARSZAŁKOWSKA ST.
UJAZDOWSKIE AVE.
MOKOTÓW

N
W E
S

0   KM   2
0   1 MILE   1

exploding shells broke out all over Żoliborz. The battle had started in earnest.

With the support of a heavy Tiger tank, the Germans attacked the building at the corner of Krasiński and Suzina Streets, so we decided to move to Żeromski Park. However, when we got to the lower part of Krasiński Street, we realized that we would have to attempt to cross it while it was being swept with tank fire. The German machine guns were placed so low that the bullets were cutting the leaves off the potato plants growing in the center strip of the boulevard.

In spite of this we had to cross the boulevard. Crouching, with my rifle in my hands, I ran at a terrific speed, but I got pinned down in the middle of the road and was unable to proceed.

Then, the tank trained the muzzle of its big gun on my position and the first shell exploded about twenty-five meters from where I was lying. The next was even nearer, so there was no time to think.

We all jumped up and with one rush covered the distance to the other side of the boulevard. While I was pinned down in the middle of the boulevard, a bullet had cut my sleeve and wounded my right arm slightly. I was very lucky, but 'Bogdan' had received a serious leg wound and we had to go back for him.

When we entered the building on the other side of the street, we left our wounded with the medics, and a nurse dressed my wound and gave me some water. As we sat in the courtyard, an old lady blessed us with the sign of the cross. She was crying with joy and excitement because the longed-for hour of the Uprising had really come at last.

As night fell the shooting stopped, and Żoliborz became quiet again; only the crackle of flames from the burning houses disturbed the silence. Gradually, however, the survivors of the dispersed units began to gather on the streets of Żoliborz, some of them coming all the way from Bielany and Powązki.

TUESDAY, AUGUST 1 NIGHT

We all regrouped and started to advance toward the building on Krasiński Street where our company was stationed. When we reached our company safely, we heard that during the day there have been heavy losses. So, our detachment has been lucky, for the only two wounded are 'Thur,' on whom a wall, struck by a shell from a Tiger tank, had collapsed, and 'Bogdan.' However, 'Wacek' is missing.

Hungry and tired, we could hardly stand, but there could be no rest for us. After a short break, the order to march put us all on our feet again. Our detachment now consisted of our leader, 'Korwin,' the deputy leader, Cadet-Officer 'Wilk,' and the following men—'Sławek'; 'Krzysztof'; 'Thur'; 'Gryf'; 'Gazda'; 'Wróbel'; 'Horodeński'; 'Chudy'; 'Lewko'; two brothers, 'Longinus' and 'Cygan'; 'Sas'; and myself, 'Goliat.'

WEDNESDAY, AUGUST 2

We started from Żoliborz around midnight in a soft drizzle and withdrew from the city toward Bielany. They said we were on the way to the Great Kampinoska Forest, which was to be the concentration point for all units fighting in the region of Żoliborz and Bielany.

Under cover of night, we succeeded in passing the German antiaircraft-gun positions without being seen, and after about an hour's good marching, we found ourselves near Bielany. By now, the rain had become a real downpour, and we were all soon soaked to the skin.

I was dressed in my father's thin uniform from the First World War, without any sweater or overcoat. Most of the others were as inadequately dressed as I was. Trembling with cold, hunger, and fatigue, and shielding my rifle under my jacket, I marched along briskly—we were in a hurry to get as far from the city as possible before daybreak.

Just after passing Bielany, 'Baron's' hand grenade exploded on his belt, making a terrible wound in his stomach. It was one of the homemade grenades which had often proved to be very unsafe.

Fragments of the grenade also wounded 'Akropolites.' 'Baron' begged us to put him out of his agony; he knew we could not take him with us, and we could not leave him for the Germans to find.

Leaving 'Baron's' body behind us, we continued our march in downcast spirits.

WEDNESDAY, AUGUST 2 MORNING

Gray wet fog dragged across the fields, hovering over the hillocks, and distorting the birches, willows, wild apple trees, and straggly junipers. In the distance loomed a ribbon of woods. We were moving across soft wet fields with high wild grasses, past slumbering hamlets, drawn toward the wilderness. There, we hoped to find safety, and time to retrieve weapons from armsdrops.

As we reached the hamlet of Sieraków, we could make out a spotter plane hovering over us, and then Colonel 'Żywiciel' gave the order for the march to end.

After placing machine-gun nests around the village and sending a few patrols out into the surrounding countryside, we threw ourselves down in a hayloft.

WEDNESDAY, AUGUST 2 AFTERNOON

After that short rest, we each got a cup of soup with potatoes from our hosts, and we gobbled it all up with great gusto. However, it only whetted our appetites, and after we had finished, we felt we would like something solid to eat, so 'Longinus' and I went to look for some food in the village.

We soon realized we were not the first, as all the hens which had managed to survive the raids of the hungry young soldiers were locked up in huts and very well guarded. We passed through the whole village without finding a hen, and only when we had reached the end of the street did we hear a sound that was like music to our ears, the squealing of a pig. We immediately entered the hut and ordered the peasant woman to take us to the animal.

The old woman, sensing that her pig was in danger, tried to tell us that her neighbor had a much bigger pig. We answered that we

205

did not need a big one. Then, eyeing the rifles on our arms, she opened the gate and we saw a lovely fat pig lying on the straw.

We aimed our rifles and 'Longinus' gave a short burst from his Sten gun; but the pig was very strong and, though bleeding, it jumped over a small wall, trying to escape into the fields.

I gave it the finishing burst.

Knowing what the pig meant to her, we paid the old woman 500 *złoty* and allowed her to cut off the head as food for her children. Then we hung the victim on a thick pole, put it on our shoulders and started on the way back to our headquarters. Needless to say, we got many jealous looks from passing soldiers on the way. Our friends, who hailed us as conquering heroes, took the pig into the hut, where we cooked it on a spit.

WEDNESDAY, AUGUST 2 NIGHT

At 11:30 tonight the whistle sounded. We all eagerly gathered together, and the cooked pig was cut up and distributed among us. We sat there, our hands full of steaming pieces of hot pork and our fingers dripping with tasty fat, and then learned that in fifteen minutes we were to start back to Warsaw.

Although we were very tired, we started on the return march with great excitement. We were going to fight the enemy and to defend our homes and families. It was raining again, but the thought that we were returning to Warsaw fortified us.

Marching past the little hamlet of Laski, we reached the village of Wólka Węglowa. There we ran straight into enemy troops. The column halted, but instead of an exchange of fire there appeared to be only an exchange of words between the advance platoon of our company and the enemy. Soon the word passed that the "enemy" was a Hungarian infantry unit, and their commanding officer had expressed a desire to talk to our officers.

The exchange took place in German, with marked Polish and Hungarian accents. Only isolated phrases reached me in the pitch darkness, as the pouring rain fell on my waterlogged hair and uniform. I heard phrases about the centuries-long friendship between Hungary and Poland, the longed-for end to the war, and of better times to come—mixed with a hardly veiled lack of sympathy for the Germans. It ended with the Hungarians giving us permission to pass unharmed. There was an exchange of salutes between the officers, and the column was on the move again. As we trooped through the puddles on the village street, the Hungarians waved, wishing us "Godspeed."

The rain was now coming down in sheets that deluged and separated us. Those responsible for finding the way often took the wrong turn. The column broke, and became longer and longer. I was worried about my rifle, which was getting wet in spite of my attempts to protect it.

THURSDAY, AUGUST 3 MORNING

At last, as we reached Wawrzyszew, the village closest to Żoliborz, the rain let up, and we began to see each other again. I had actually been asleep as I automatically moved my legs—I had never believed until now that it is possible to march in a semiconscious state. Only when I was tripped by a protruding, gnarled tree root, or lurched into the man in front of me, had I awakened.

The stillness of the dawn found us in an open field. A group of officers stood against the wooden fence surrounding a homestead; in the morning mist, Colonel 'Żywiciel' and his staff were probably discussing what to do with their wet troops, caught by the daylight in the middle of a compound of straw-roofed wooden houses.

In the distance, through the haze, the outlines of the Workers' Conquest Housing Colony near Bielany were beginning to emerge. Situated in the triangle of roads between Bielany, Żoliborz, and Wawrzyszew, the Colony presented the only feasible hiding place. If spotted in Wawrzyszew, our column would be quickly destroyed by artillery stationed in nearby Powązki.

Lieutenant 'Szymura' passed me on his way to the 230th Platoon, which formed the advance guard.

The column then reached the Workers' Conquest Colony and we were ordered to take up positions in the apartment blocks and surrounding individual houses.

Although the enemy was at the Bielany airfield with antiaircraft artillery and in the Central Institute of Physical Education with crack SS troops, we were in a good humor. We had had breakfast, and now we were cleaning our weapons and getting ready to take up positions at the windows of the house in which our detachment was stationed.

A long field spread out before us, reaching to Żoliborz on the right, and on the left running as far as a few blocks of houses, which gave us some measure of protection against the battalions of the *Waffen* SS housed in the Institute, and also from the barracks of the German airmen at the airfield. Nevertheless, there was serious danger here for all of us, and we got strict instructions from Colonel 'Żywiciel' not to fire without a direct order from him so as not to disclose our positions prematurely.

At 8:00 A.M., a patrol came out into the open field from behind the opposite blocks of houses. It consisted of eight *Luftwaffe* men, carrying machine guns and rifles.

They walked fairly slowly, talking among themselves, apparently unaware that hundreds of us were positioned here. Only when they were about 110 meters from our positions did they start to pay more attention and advance in line formation.

We all felt frustrated at being unable to fire at them, but the order was clear. However, when the Germans were about thirty-five meters from our location, a shot was fired from a distant house on our left. The Germans withdrew, but took every opportunity to fire back.

Finally, we got the actual order to fire, and those of us who were within range immediately shot at the retreating Germans. Lieutenant 'Szajer' was kneeling at the window from which I was firing. His second shot wounded the leader of the patrol, a *Luftwaffe* sergeant, who fell to the ground badly hurt and moaned with pain for the next hour until he died.

Now that our positions were discovered, we had to prepare to defend them. After about an hour, another German patrol came out, twice as strong as the one before and with more light machine guns. However, because men in only some of the houses had fired on the first German patrol, the second patrol clearly expected to find us rather few in number. They had, therefore, sent only about twenty men to take us.

This time they started to advance from the beginning in skirmish formation. They advanced in a series of dashes, firing at our windows with their machine guns and rifles.

A hail of bullets entered the windows behind which we were taking cover, shattering the tiles of the stove in the room. Incendiary bullets set the sofa and the carpet on fire, but we soon stopped it from spreading.

After a few minutes, the German fire was returned from more and more houses, and finally, after half an hour's shooting, the Germans began to withdraw, taking shelter behind the small sandy hillocks in the field.

THURSDAY, AUGUST 3 MIDDAY

While preparing the defense, Colonel 'Żywiciel' had given our Commando company—the only one really armed—the job of securing the outposts. The 226th, my platoon, and the 229th Platoon were ordered to take up positions opposite each other in the rows of individual houses on Żeromski Street. A patrol was also sent to nearby Kleczewska Street in order to seize a house there and then to wait for the next order. Members of our detachment were selected for the patrol. I was among them, and 'Korwin' was our leader.

After a careful examination of our Sten guns and rifles, we proceeded—under cover of the gardens—to carry out our task. Creeping along, we crossed a road which was under enemy machine-gun fire and then found ourselves at the designated house. The frightened inhabitants had already spent the whole morning in the cellar; when they saw us, armed to the teeth, they left the place altogether.

After we had explored the house, 'Korwin' placed a few of us at the windows as observers. We were to be relieved every two hours in order to break the monotony. With hand grenades stuck in his sapper's boots, and a semiautomatic rifle nonchalantly slung across his shoulders, the bearded 'Korwin' gave the impression of a pirati-

209

cal guerrilla rather than of a well-disciplined junior officer. Then, our "heroic" leader stationed himself in the cellar, from where he gave us his orders. I was placed behind the window of the large and still beautifully furnished living room.

The machine-gun volleys and shells exploded constantly. Every five minutes or so a bullet or fragment of a mortar shell would enter the room and strike the furniture or the walls. Then there came an unexpected letup and, crouching below the window, I found time at last to think.

I thought of Ludwik in particular. We finally were doing what he had dreamed of for four long years. We were in the thick of battle against the Occupier—and the man who had brought me into the fight, who had steeped all of us in the need to fight and perhaps die for freedom, was not there. I hoped he would have been pleased with the results of his careful and constant planning to turn young boys into fighting soldiers.

The maneuvers of the Third of May, deep in the Great Kampinoska Forest, in about the same spot where we had been the previous night, the visit to the Fighting Ghetto, the faces of Ola, Stefa, Zula—all passed before my eyes in swift succession.

I wondered where the Uprising found my father, and how he, my mother, and my sister were managing. Marysia, I somehow knew, was all right, and I felt strongly that if I managed only to survive this day, I would see her again.

While I was thus deep in thought and feeling very uncomfortable on the hard floor, I turned onto my other side and then noticed on the piano a photograph of a very beautiful girl. The face seemed very familiar to me.

After a moment I was sure it was the likeness of my cousin, Ania Marjańska, who lived in Komorów, near Warsaw. I soon remembered that one of her family had a house on this street and thought, here I am now, I do not know why, in that very house.

THURSDAY, AUGUST 3 AFTERNOON

In the afternoon, all hell broke loose. The artillery, tanks, and heavy mortars fell on our positions at the Workers' Conquest Colony. Occasionally a Tiger tank passed along the next street, or even along ours, sometimes so close to the house that it nearly touched the walls. The whole earth trembled with heavy explosions and we could hear the voices of the advancing Germans quite plainly. Every minute they could be heard more clearly, and we soon found ourselves in the middle of the German infantry and tank units attacking the Workers' Conquest Colony.

We were now in a hopeless position, well behind enemy lines. If we were discovered by the Germans, we would not be able to defend ourselves for more than a few minutes. We could not even hope to get any help from our company, as we were completely cut off from them.

Then 'Korwin'—who was as intelligent as he was cautious—found a small door behind a locker in the cellar which led to a tiny hiding place under the stairs. After removing all traces of our stay in the house, he ordered us to go in there one after another. We pulled the locker back in place from inside so that nobody could detect the door from the outside.

The hiding place was very tiny, only as long as the height of an average man and little more than one and a half meters at its highest point. It is incredible how such a small hole could hold nine men, three of them very tall.

We were all sitting so that each man's head was resting against the back of the man in front, our knees drawn up to our chins. We clung firmly to our precious weapons, and tried to ignore the growling of our empty stomachs. In this extremely uncomfortable position, nearly suffocating from the lack of fresh air, stiff and cramped, we waited.

All the time the battle continued in its full fury and we could hear the voices of the Germans outside our building. The thought that our friends were fighting and dying while we were sitting under the stairs and doing nothing, caused us anguish and frustration, but we had no choice.

While waiting for the Germans, we decided that, if attacked, we were going to fight to the end and then explode our hand grenades rather than be captured alive. Every one of us agreed on that point.

By the end of the day, the roar of the battle ceased and we no longer heard German voices. After six hours of unimaginable physical contortions, we were at last able to leave our hiding place and to get some fresh air into our lungs. None of us would ever forget those six hours.

THURSDAY, AUGUST 3   NIGHT

As we had already spent a long time in the house without receiving any orders, 'Korwin' decided that we should go back, under cover of night, and find out what had happened to the rest of our troops.

On the way, we could see that the Workers' Conquest Colony was in flames. The houses were almost unrecognizable, only some walls and chimneys were left.

Freedom Fighters

Here and there big holes had been bored in the gardens by the shells of the German heavy artillery, and sometimes we saw the mutilated bodies of our comrades—the victims of a murderous battle. Wounded were lying in the gardens in front of the houses, being tended to and comforted by our ever-courageous nurses.

When we reached our company, 'Korwin' reported to the Company Commander. After a very hearty welcome from our friends, we were given the names of our companions who had been killed or wounded, a growing list. We were also told about the battle.

During that day our units had incurred terrible casualties; the poorly built houses could not protect our soldiers against artillery or tank fire. Our company, in particular, had suffered great losses. Among the officers, the Deputy Company Commander, Lieutenant 'Szymura,' had been seriously wounded, receiving his third hit in two days of fighting. Nevertheless, he commanded his platoon to the very end. Another of our platoons, the 230th, suffered especially heavy casualties during a counterattack on the attacking Germans—losing seventeen men.

'Kalisz's' detachment had been pinned down between the tanks and the attacking infantry. 'Jerzy' was one of the heavily wounded from that detachment. Young 'Ewa,' one of the company's nurses, ran into the middle of the machine-gun crossfire. Somehow, she reached the wounded man and, with the help of a couple of soldiers, pulled him from the field, and saw that he was put on a stretcher at the back of one of the houses. There, he and the brave nurse were killed by an artillery shell.

There was no end to the stories of individual sacrifice during this first battle in the open.

Because we had not taken part in much of the day's fighting, we were not as exhausted as the others, so our detachment was ordered to go onto the battlefield to gather arms and ammunition from the dead. We moved quietly among the sand dunes, which were dimly lit by the moon. Every few meters there was a dead body, lying twisted in every possible position, generally a soldier of our company. I came up to one of them who was lying on his face, his rifle still locked tightly in his hands. I pulled the rifle out of his lifeless grasp. He had been killed by a bullet which had passed through his helmet and into his forehead. I also took his helmet away, because helmets were priceless possessions. I washed it out later in cold water, but because it was too small for me, I passed it on to 'Lewko.'

About 300 meters from our positions, German corpses were lying—those who had died from our bullets—young and old Germans, torn, twisted and covered with blood, sleeping peacefully for the first time in a long while.

The field of death made the deepest impression on me; it was the first time I had seen so many fragmented bodies and horrible gaping wounds. Yet, I followed orders and collected helmets, arms, and ammunition.

Soon Colonel 'Żywiciel' moved all our forces toward Żoliborz, leaving the wounded in the care of the inhabitants of Bielany and sending soldiers without weapons back to the Great Kampinoska Forest. We started out at eleven o'clock at night but it took us over two hours to cover that short distance, as the Germans were sweeping the fields with searchlights and rockets, so that we had to stop and lie immobile every few minutes.

If the Germans had noticed our units in the middle of the field, their heavy artillery would not have left any of us alive. Fortunately, we passed the enemy's artillery positions safely, by taking our shoes off and even trying not to breathe. About 350 of us safely reached Żoliborz.

We were billeted in numerous houses, and for the first time in several days had a roof under which to sleep. We were looked after by the civilians, who helped us in every way they could.

Thus, we regained Żoliborz again, promising to defend it and its inhabitants to the last drop of our blood.

FRIDAY, AUGUST 4

Much of Warsaw is ours again! In many areas, the red and white flag of Poland is flying over the scarred but proud city for the first time in almost five years, and the hated swastikas have been torn down and burned.

Since early this morning, the civilian population has been working with the army in building barricades and in digging anti-tank and communications trenches throughout Żoliborz. The barricades consist of everything imaginable: overturned streetcars, all types of furniture from nearby houses, garbage cans, even mounds of trash. Some of the barricades are so high that they reach up to the second floors of adjacent buildings.

The civilians are really eager to help, and work on the fortifications is proceeding swiftly and exceedingly well. The life of the citi-

A 1944 Uprising poster: EVERY BULLET MUST COUNT!

zens has been quickly "normalized" since the enemy withdrew to the perimeter of Żoliborz.

The *Wehrmacht* and SS formations are quartered in fortified strongholds—in the Chemical Institute at the top of Polish Army Avenue, the southwest corner of the area held by us; on both sides of the Warsaw–Gdańsk Railway viaduct to the south; in the Old Citadel, and along the banks of the Vistula in the east; in the old Chemical Warfare School in Marymont in the north; in the public school building on Kolektorska Street; and in the Central Institute of Physical Education in the northwest.

We hold a large area, but it is strangled by the railroad line to the south and west, the banks of the Vistula to the east, and the Bielany Forest to the north.

The land which seems to be defended the most heavily by the Germans is the area along both sides of the Warsaw–Gdańsk Rail-

215

Sentry

Communication Trench

way Line, which cuts us off from the rest of those parts of the city which have been liberated. From a military point of view, our separation from the group holding the Old City is particularly unfortunate.

The only "reliable" means of communication between Żoliborz and the Old City is through the underground sewer pipes. At the same time, the residential streets of Żoliborz lead to woods and fields in the northeast and provide a link with the Great Kampinoska Forest and, through it, with the rest of the country.

After cleaning our weapons, and dressing the cuts and bruises acquired during our march in the rain to and from the Great Kampinoska Forest, we remain in a state of constant alert. We are stationed in three-story apartment buildings on Suzina Street, and new red and white armbands have been distributed among us, with

The Center City

Barricade

The Flag of Freedom

The Flag of Defeat

The Detachment:
top row, from left:
*The author ('Goliat'),
'Wilk,' and 'Wróbel.'*
Middle row, from left:
*'Cygan,' 'Nick,'
'Gazda,' and 'Sławek.'*
Bottom row:
'Krzysztof.'

The Author

A Signal Corps Messenger and Sentry

the number of each platoon stamped on them. The stamps are meant to prevent unauthorized use of the armbands, which are more important than ever for quick identification now that so many of us are wearing captured German helmets and parts of uniforms.

We pass the time talking to the nurses, who eagerly listen to the story of yesterday's battles. I have my share of such attention. One girl frequently comes to our quarters, usually with her arms full of food, as she knows how short we are of rations.

But although I am most popular and my friends are quite jealous at the attention I receive, I have been looking forward to seeing only one person, who to my great pleasure has come at last. Marysia! Somehow she has found out where we are. She looks so warm, beautiful, and human, that the mere sight of her brings a glow to my heart.

But soon all our visitors are leaving. From early this afternoon heavy artillery fire has fallen on our immediate area, so our company has received an order to move into the cellar, where the inhabitants of the building are already sheltering. Waiting there, our detachment is disclosing a previously hidden talent. In the midst of exploding artillery shells, we have started to sing; the rest of the company, and the occupants of the cellar, are listening enraptured. The cellar is ringing with such songs as: "Storm Company," "Little Lieutenant," "A Kiss Is as Sweet as a Date," "Unfaithful Mary," and many other soldiers' songs. Our detachment now plans to sing our company anthem, written by 'Korwin.'

SATURDAY, AUGUST 5

Two detachments of our platoon were called to the still unfinished barricade at Słowacki Street today, to defend it against the attacking German infantry. We repelled three enemy attacks with our hand grenades and with our machine guns, Sten guns, and rifles. In this action, eighteen were killed on the German side while we had only two wounded.

While we were engaged in this counterattack, the 229th Platoon was fighting against troops supported by a tank, attacking from the river toward Wilson Square. The 230th Platoon fought with an enemy patrol on Krasiński Street. This day brought us complete victory, as the German attacks were repelled everywhere.

We are not far from Feliński Street, and this evening Aunt Stacha (informed by Marysia that I was here) came to our quarters, dust-covered and tired but bringing some wine and food from home. Aunt Stacha tells me that my father is now in the Old City of Warsaw, with the General Staff of the Home Army, and that this part of the city is presently under the heaviest fire.

The Germans are attacking the Old City with airplanes, tanks, infantry, and all available artillery. From Żoliborz one can see quite plainly the dreadful pall of smoke hanging over the Old City, and hear the unceasing explosions of bombs and artillery shells. Every hour enemy *Stukas* fly over Żoliborz from the Bielany airfield, dropping bombs on the city before returning for a new assault. It is outright slaughter; we do not have one antiaircraft gun in the entire city.

According to the news circulating in Żoliborz, the enemy is now fighting to open an artery from the western part of Warsaw through the Center City held by the Home Army, all the way across the river to the eastern suburb of Praga. The reason is obvious. The German Army fighting the Red Army across the river has lost its vital line of supply, which we have cut. Unless they can restore contact, they will not be able to hold out against the Soviet troops much longer. Therefore, they are throwing their main forces against the Home Army units blocking their way. We hear that a brigade of Ukrainians, organized by the Germans from Soviet war prisoners with promises of plunder, food, and vodka, is fighting with the Germans.

The westernmost suburb of Wola evidently has received the brunt of the first attack, and it is reported that the Germans and Ukrainians are giving no quarter to anyone in their way. They are taking no prisoners, and are killing men, women, and children on sight. According to eyewitnesses who have reached Żoliborz, the entire staff (as well as the sick and wounded) at the Hospital of Saint Lazar on Leszno Street has been massacred. Babies were swung by the legs and their heads split on the corners of buildings; women were raped before being shot; and hundreds of civilians

221

were herded by the Germans in front of tanks attacking the barricades. Polish fighters cannot open fire on these innocent civilian shields, and some of the enemy's successes have been due to this tactic.

Were it not for what has happened during the last few years, and what happened to the Ghetto little more than a year ago, nobody would have believed the Germans capable of such barbarism.

SS Gruppenführer *Heinz Reinefarth directing his brigade's operations*

SATURDAY, AUGUST 5   NIGHT

By nightfall, 'Żywiciel' gave our company the job of holding the northernmost area of Żoliborz, the most exposed of our defenses. The 229th and 230th Platoons have been assigned to protect our northeastern flank, and are to provide our platoon with reinforcements as needed. They are located off Słowacki Street.

Our platoon has been chosen to take over and hold the Fire Brigade Building, my old fire-fighting headquarters, at the junction of Potocki and Słowacki Streets. It is a most dangerous location, as it has put us forward of our own lines, and means that we are surrounded by the enemy's positions. But the Germans will not expect us to be in the building, for they are not likely to believe that we would try to occupy an area so near their strongholds. We had to make our way here under machine-gun and mortar fire from the old Chemical Warfare School, which the enemy holds. We crawled all the way under cover of the very dark night. When we reached the building, I was able to explain its layout to my comrades. After setting up observation posts at several windows and taking all possible precautions, we went to sleep in the dormitories previously used by the firemen.

SUNDAY, AUGUST 6 MORNING

We were all careful not to appear at the windows, even during the night. The morning passed very peacefully, and it was not until about eleven that our observer informed us that the enemy was advancing from the direction of Bielany.

We soon took our positions behind the windows, and just when we had finished placing our platoon's three light machine guns we saw a German truck racing down Słowacki Street. When the unsuspecting truck was about 225 meters from our building, we fired. Unfortunately, our shots went wild and the Germans quickly turned their truck around and escaped at full speed. We were furious with ourselves because we had disclosed our positions.

During the night, 'Szajer' had sent one of our detachments to the Health Center across Słowacki Street. This building was of strategic importance to us, for if the Germans tried to attack us, they would be caught in a crossfire from us and the detachment on duty at the Health Center.

SUNDAY, AUGUST 6 AFTERNOON

At about noon, a fast-firing field gun arrived from the direction of Bielany and, after being placed about 350 meters from our building, it opened fire. The crew's task was clearly to ascertain whether the building was still occupied. After half an hour's firing, the Germans withdrew the gun, evidently deciding we were not in the building since they had not drawn our fire.

A German Field Gun

A few minutes later, however, our building received another burst of shells. This time the enemy used their heavy artillery, and the bombardment was heavy and long. Our lieutenant gave an order for us to remain at our positions, although our people were being wounded right and left by enemy shells.

One of the shells exploded on a corridor wall just over 'Szajer's' head, knocking him down and covering him with bricks. I saw the explosion from the other end of the corridor and thought him dead. But after a few minutes he got up from under the rubble and staggered over to us. His escape was miraculous; except for a few bad bruises, he was not even injured.

In the meantime, one of the observation posts had reported an enemy skirmishing party advancing toward our positions. It was now around 2:00 P.M. The Germans, who had noticed that we had remained silent all through the day, began to advance more boldly and we could soon hear their officers shouting commands.

We learned that they wanted to attack the barricade situated some 275 meters behind our positions. We saw about 350 Germans preparing for the attack. Our platoon consisted of only about 40 men, but we were determined to fight to the end when the time came.

A Sharpshooter

The Germans approached our building and, after passing it, started the attack on the barricade. They soon realized that they had their hands full, and, since they were under continuous fire from the neighboring blocks of houses, they started to move slowly backwards. Only a few of them remained, firing at the barricade with their machine guns.

Then came the long-awaited order to fire. We put the muzzles of our rifles, Sten guns, and machine guns forward through the windows, and poured a murderous fire down on the Germans, who were taken completely by surprise. In addition to this, the detachment on duty at the Health Center lost no time in firing on the enemy from the other side and launching an attack. One after another, the Germans were struck down by our bullets.

Positioned immediately under the window from which I was firing was an SS police machine-gun squad. At the first burst from Cadet-Officer 'Zawada's' Sten gun a machine-gunner was shot down. Although he was badly wounded, he tried to retreat, spitting blood and leaving a deadly red trail on the pavement. A rifle shot finished him off. He fell spread-eagled in the gutter. A few meters from him another policeman was lying with his stomach torn open by bullets. We did not spare ammunition when shooting at SS policemen—the men who had been responsible for the slaughter in the Ghetto, for the executions, the street hunts, and the wanton murders.

The retreating enemy stopped just beyond our field of fire and brought their fast-firing gun and heavy machine gun to bear on our positions. It seemed they were attempting to prevent us from picking up weapons from their fallen comrades. However, our troops were poorly armed, and some were without arms at all, so we were much too tempted by weapons lying in the middle of the boulevard to be stopped.

Some of us crawled into the middle of the street between bursting shells to collect the arms. 'Longinus' had spotted a large machine pistol next to an SS policeman. He managed to get it, and under heavy machine-gun fire returned to our building. After being pinned down by machine-gun fire in the middle of Słowacki Street, I returned, scratched but unharmed—crawling all the way

—with an automatic rifle in my hand. But the enemy's gunfire had left my uniform in shreds.

During the fight, we captured twenty rifles, two machine pistols, and one machine gun. Three SS policemen were taken prisoner.

The bodies of four of the enemy were lying in the middle of the square in front of our building, and one of them lay very near their own positions. Under cover of night, but still within range of bullets from enemy machine guns, we pulled the blood-smeared corpses away with ropes in order to take the arms and ammunition from them.

My shoes were falling apart after the long march to and from the Great Kampinoska Forest. I took a pair of boots from one of the bodies and, as they fitted, I put them on.

In addition to all the losses suffered by our platoon in battle, during the arms-cleaning hour 'Wilk' was accidentally wounded in the leg by one of our own soldiers. This unfortunate accident has not only caused 'Wilk' a great deal of pain but has also put him out of action.

MONDAY, AUGUST 7

Today has passed in the usual tiresome guard duties; we are still under steady artillery fire but occasionally are able to shoot at an enemy car or truck passing near our building. We have to break the monotony somehow.

We have been told that while we are defending Żoliborz, the Germans are concentrating their main effort on breaking through the area from Wola to the Saski Gardens, Brühl Palace, then to Kierbedzia Bridge, and on to Praga. This attempt to gain an east-west corridor to the Russian Front, however, has run into fierce opposition. In spite of countless brutal sorties by the Germans, every barricade, every house, and every square foot of land is being fiercely defended.

City Hall under fire

TUESDAY, AUGUST 8

The wedge of German steel today succeeded in advancing along Elektoralna Street to Brühl Palace, where Fischer and his staff have been surrounded since the first shot of the Uprising was fired on Suzina Street. Isolated in his fortress palace, defended by his Storm Troopers and select SS units, the Governor has been locked in a precarious position, not knowing when an attempt might be made to capture him. Fischer can have no illusions as to what will happen to him if he falls into our hands.

Today we heard a few details of what is happening there. Three days ago, General Erich von dem Bach took over as Commander-in-Chief of all German units. Soon after that, Home Army units surrounding Brühl Palace were pushed back, and von dem Bach sent Fischer instructions to leave the Palace as soon as possible. Von dem Bach, charged personally by Hitler not to take prisoners, to kill women and children as well as civilian men, and to eradicate the city of Warsaw from the face of the earth, had been anxious to get Fischer out as soon as he arrived in Wola, the westerly suburb.

The Enemy

The next day, around ten o'clock in the morning, under heavy guard, and with the protection of armored cars, Fischer's entire staff started to leave the Palace. As they were attempting the get-away, our units made a surprise attack. It was totally unexpected as the route was heavily guarded on both sides by thousands of German troops brought in earlier to push back the Home Army.

In the attack, the *Gruppenführer* was wounded, and several members of his entourage were either killed or wounded.

SATURDAY, AUGUST 12

We have been holding on to our positions in the Fire Brigade Building for several seemingly interminable days under steady artillery fire. At about 11:00 A.M. today, a German truck was seen racing toward our building. This time we allowed it to come closer than before, and when it was about forty-five meters from us, we stopped it with our fire. The Germans immediately jumped out. One of them was killed, but the other two managed to get away. The truck remained in the open space which was now under continuous cross fire.

Then Cadet-Officer 'Zawada,' along with two others, ran to the truck and succeeded in bringing it to the garage doors at the front of our building, although they were shot at by a German machine gun.

As he was under fire all the time, it did not surprise us when 'Zawada' crashed the right wheel against the corner of the garage wall. The truck was full of wooden crates, and opening one, we found it full of German hand grenades. We were overjoyed at our luck and started to unload the crates as quickly as possible, as we knew that the Germans would press their attack even harder now. Sure enough, just as we were putting the last crate in the cellar, the whole building shook from the explosion of an artillery shell, which had hit the fifth floor.

Now a dreadful time started for us. Shell after shell began to explode in the different rooms and the gunpowder made our eyes smart—sometimes the explosions were so close that the shock waves threw us against the walls. The entire building's rooms and corridors were covered in clouds of dust, and strewn with pieces of brick and fragments of exploded shells.

But the observers held their original places and paid extra attention in case the infantry advanced behind the screen of the artillery barrage. The firing only stopped with the coming of night. We were then able to take three seriously wounded men to a hospital and dress on the spot the wounds of those less badly injured.

Our building is now so perforated from the outside that it looks like a Swiss cheese, and inside all the rooms are badly damaged. We can only manage three to four hours' sleep each night, as we have to spend time at the observation posts, clean our weapons, and check our ammunition.

SUNDAY, AUGUST 13

Today's issue of our new newspaper, the *Żoliborz Daily*, carries a report about the capture of the four thousand hand grenades by the 226th Platoon. It also mentions that they are being distributed to all the Żoliborz platoons.

Freedom Fighters, 1944 Uprising

Freedom Fighters, 1944 Uprising

A Polish officer, 1944 Uprising

WEDNESDAY, AUGUST 16

After ten days of exhausting duty at the Fire Brigade Building, our company has been relieved and sent away from the front line for a short rest.

The building on Mickiewicz Street (between Inwalidów and Wilson Squares) where our company is now quartered is one of the few apartment houses which, at least up to now, has not been either bombed or fired upon by enemy artillery. Here, for the first time in almost a month, I will be able to sleep in a bed and to enjoy edible food.

THURSDAY, AUGUST 17

The strain of the last few weeks, the exhaustion and hunger, have finally all caught up with me. I am running a high fever and am so weak that I cannot get out of bed. The owners of one of the apartments are kindly looking after me, and dear Aunt Stacha, notified by them, has been to visit me and bring me food.

232

SATURDAY, AUGUST 19

Tonight, after two days of nursing by my hosts, I felt my fever subsiding and got up to join them in the evening meal. Their young cousin, a courier who only the day before had made a harrowing trip through the sewers, was at the table. She brought an important message from Colonel 'Wachnowski' in the Old City. The whole evening was spent listening to the news of other parts of the city from which we were cut off.

While we were tied down in Żoliborz, fighting off individual attacks, the rest of the city had been going through veritable hell. The Russians were withdrawing from the outskirts of Warsaw after refusing to help us in any way. In fact, information reaching General Bór-Komorowski's headquarters told of his officers being arrested by the Red Army, as they carried out his order to bring all armed units of the Home Army into Warsaw through the Great Kampinoska Forest.

SUNDAY, AUGUST 20

As the Germans began to launch yet another attack on the Old City today, two of our officers made their way to Żoliborz through the fetid sewers, with orders for the newly arrived Partisan units from eastern Poland who had come to Żoliborz through the Great Kampinoska Forest.

The orders were for the Partisans to attempt to break through the German lines in order to replenish the depleted garrison forces in the Old City. In spite of the courage and the dedication of the Partisans, however, the attack has failed and nearly one hundred dead and wounded soldiers now lie in the field in front of the Warsaw–Gdańsk Railway Station.

MONDAY, AUGUST 21

General 'Grzegorz' and Colonel 'Heller' have reached Żoliborz after a tortuous trip through the fast-flowing sewers. They are here to organize a full-scale attack. This time it is to be coordinated with a joint attack from the other side of the railway line. Our com-

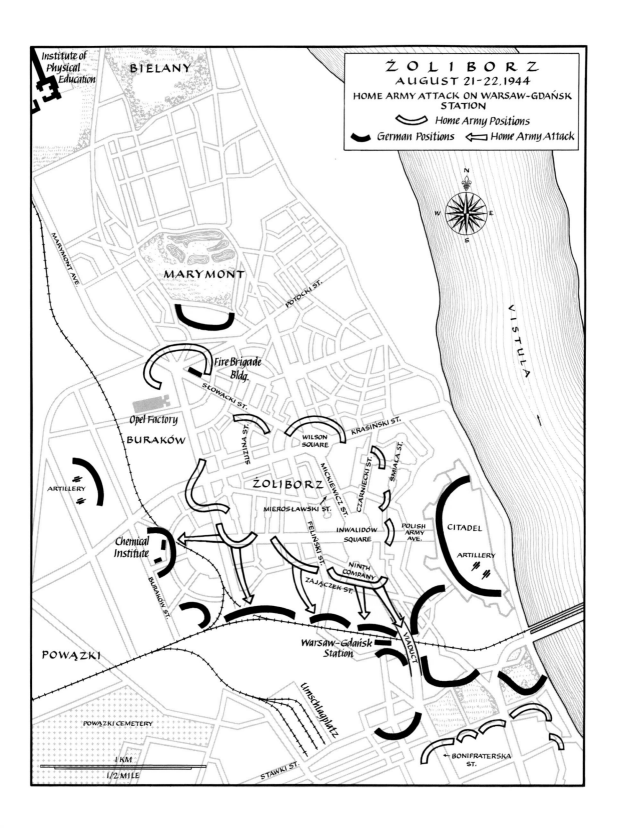

ŻOLIBORZ
AUGUST 21-22, 1944
HOME ARMY ATTACK ON WARSAW-GDAŃSK
STATION
Home Army Positions
German Positions   Home Army Attack

Institute of Physical Education

BIELANY

MARYMONT

VISTULA

MARYMONT AVE.

POTOCKI ST.

Fire Brigade Bldg.

SŁOWACKI ST.

Opel Factory

BURAKÓW

SUZINA ST.

WILSON SQUARE

KRASIŃSKI ST.

ŻOLIBORZ

MICKIEWICZ ST.

CZARNIECKI ST.

ŚMIAŁA ST.

MIEROSŁAWSKI ST.

ARTILLERY

INWALIDÓW SQUARE

POLISH ARMY AVE.

CITADEL

ARTILLERY

Chemical Institute

FELIŃSKI ST.

NINTH COMPANY

BURAKÓW ST.

ZAJĄCZEK ST.

VIADUCT

POWĄZKI

Warsaw-Gdańsk Station

Umschlagplatz

BONIFRATERSKA ST.

POWĄZKI CEMETERY

1 KM
1/2 MILE

STAWKI ST.

pany's mission is to attack the Warsaw–Gdańsk Station itself, thus diverting the attention of the enemy from other sections of the line —and permitting the Partisans to reach the Old City. Almost the entire force of Żoliborz, under the personal command of Colonel 'Żywiciel,' is assembled along the full length of the line from the Old Citadel to the Chemical Institute and the artillery positions in the suburb of Buraków.

The night is unseasonably cold and the ground upon which we are lying is very damp. Our thin, worn-out summer clothes, now in rags, give us little protection. Our boots are covered with rags to muffle the sound of our feet on the pavement during the initial attack.

The field is regularly lit up by huge blinding flares, and the quiet is interrupted by long salvos of machine-gun fire, which cut down the grass and the potato plants around us. After the previous night's attack, the German and Ukrainian troops are jittery and trigger-happy. They are ready for us.

TUESDAY, AUGUST 22

At 2:00 A.M. the order came. We started across the street and through the previously cut openings in the lines of gnarled barbed wire, but before all our detachments could cross the street, the wide expanse of sky was lit by hundreds of marker flares. The red stars hung for a long time, casting an eerie light on the troops pinned down in the shadows of the houses.

Hundreds of shells from automatic weapons now began to rain down on Zajączek Street, while tracer bullets created a barrier of fire above the prostrate army. They spattered against the walls of the apartment houses, throwing chunks of white stucco on the black pavement, while artillery shells gouged out craters, churning up the macadam, concrete, earth, and plants.

As soon as the machine guns of our company started up, the enemy firepower began to center upon them, silencing them one by one. Our platoon advanced up to the viaduct. One boy reached a high point and threw grenades down into a heavy machine-gun nest, silencing it forever. Then, caught in the cross-fire from other machine-gun nests, he rolled back down the embankment to his starting point.

The cries of the wounded could be heard above the machine guns' rattling and the explosions, and the combat nurses crossed the road in a vain attempt to bring help. Those who could started withdrawing as the order was passed along the field. The short battle was lost.

When the enemy stopped firing, and the artillery shells from the Citadel stopped thumping, only white flares remained and bathed the field with ghostly light, illuminating the 300 dead and wounded that were left behind.

WEDNESDAY, AUGUST 23

Those attacking from the other side of the railway line, led by Major 'Bolek,' had to withdraw at dawn yesterday after an equally hard fight and with many casualties.

Our company endured particularly heavy losses, and we were all very upset to learn that the head of the nurses' section in our platoon was killed. 'Mitis' was a middle-aged woman who, although wounded herself, went into the battle line to dress the wounds of our soldiers. She had already lost her husband in Auschwitz, and her two sons had been executed by the Germans. She met her death when she was hit a second time—a dum-dum bullet struck her in the back.

Cadet-Officer 'Mirski,' who had led the patrol in which I took part on the first day of the Uprising, was also killed during this attack. Sadly, his body lay so close to the enemy's positions that it could not be recovered.

Among the wounded was a friend of mine, 'Gryf,' who lives in the apartment house in which our company is stationed at this time. His mother, who had already lost her husband to an execution squad, heard that her son was dying in the hospital. He had been seriously wounded in the stomach and died after thirty-six hours of awful pain. He became delirious in the last hour and screamed, "Attack, boys, attack—avenge my father." Lieutenant 'Szajer,' our platoon leader, got a very bad leg wound.

236

THURSDAY, AUGUST 24

Our platoon has been taken over by Cadet-Officer 'Tadeusz' who, with his detachment, joined our platoon at the beginning of the Uprising. He used to belong to Special Groups, and has participated in many of the most famous actions of the Home Army. He is definitely the best leader we could have after 'Szajer.'

FRIDAY, AUGUST 25

This morning I visited 'Bogdan,' who is still in the hospital. Then in the afternoon Aunt Stacha brought me the news that my father escaped from the Old City to Żoliborz through sewer pipes, and is

German prisoners of war, Center City

now in bed at home. His legs were badly cut by the barbed-wire coils the Germans have laid in many of the tunnels, and these cuts are now infected from the raw sewage. I immediately asked for a pass so that I could go and see him.

SUNDAY, AUGUST 27

The Old City is now a pile of rubble. We hear General Bór-Komorowski has left it today, escaping through the sewers to the Center City; he has ordered us to hold on so that other areas can continue to fight, until help arrives from the Soviet armies across the Vistula—a forlorn hope.

MONDAY, AUGUST 28

Today, Monday, our company went on duty at Colonel 'Żywiciel's' headquarters, situated on Krasiński Street near Wilson Square. During the morning, the barricade on Słowacki Street was damaged by German and Ukrainian fire, and 'Thur' and I were ordered to get a party of German prisoners of war to repair it. We collected some spades and went down to where the military police were holding the prisoners. They were eating lunch. While 'Thur' gave his orders to the sergeant, I had a chance to look at these Germans who were our prisoners. They all looked tired, dejected, and nervous. Among them were two who looked about our age, one blond and the other red-haired. We ordered the prisoners to take a spade each and to fall into line. I led this column, and 'Thur' brought up the rear.

The blond and the redhead began to mumble and stagger like a couple of drunks. Then they suddenly broke ranks and started running toward the rear of the column. I had hardly swung my rifle on them when I saw that they had fallen at 'Thur's' feet. The other prisoners looked on apprehensively, and 'Thur' looked startled. I asked one of the older prisoners, who had Russian campaign stripes, "What the hell is going on?" The prisoner was silent. Then he stepped forward and, looking down at his worn-out boots, said, "They are begging you not to kill them; they think we are being taken to dig our own graves with these spades."

A Stuka

We were disgusted and told everyone to get back into line. Then we marched them off to the damaged barricade where the military police sergeant put them to work.

THURSDAY, AUGUST 31

Żoliborz is under unrelenting bombardment. On this sunny afternoon, countless enemy *Stuka* dive-bombers flew over our positions and over Wilson Square. As they were not fired upon, they swooped low over the roofs of the apartment houses, and one could easily see the huge bombs attached to their fuselages. I saw them dive over the lower part of Mickiewicz Street. After a few minutes, a dreadful explosion shook Żoliborz, and a terrible sight met my eyes.

A German missile launcher

A German missile being loaded

Wall after wall of the enormous apartment building at 34–36 Mickiewicz Street began to fall down. The front wall of the building slipped out at the base, as a result of the well-aimed bombs, exposing all the interior floors.

After a while, a curtain of dust began to descend over the whole building. My heart sank—it was the building in which Marysia lived. My first thought was to run over there to help. But I was not allowed to leave our quarters. Later, though, an order from our commandant sent us off: "Detachment to dig up the ruins, at the double."

He did not have to tell us twice!

I started first, and forgetting military discipline, I left my detachment behind. Fear of what might have happened to my friend made my heart thump even faster than the exertion did.

Fortunately, the wing of the building where Marysia lived was still reasonably intact, but the entire middle part had collapsed onto the cellar in which the inhabitants of the building were gathered. The bombs had been dropped aslant and exploded nearly at the foot of the building.

Some rescue squads were already at the place, together with Colonel 'Żywiciel' and our Company Commander Lieutenant 'Szeliga.' Along with the others, I began to dig under the rubble. We could hear the groans of the victims buried under the broken bricks and glass.

241

A direct hit

After an hour, we succeeded in digging out a middle-aged woman whose legs were smashed and twisted. Before she lost consciousness, she whispered through pale, blood-covered lips that about ten other people had been with her before the bombs fell.

Now we began to notice a head, a leg, or an arm under the debris—a sign that we were coming to more bodies. The next to be uncovered was a man, but he was already dead, his body damaged almost beyond recognition.

After three hours of intense digging, we found a woman holding a baby in her arms. The baby wailed like a wounded bird, and its mother, though injured herself, clasped her child tightly. She lay in a very difficult position, so it took a long time to free her.

Soon after that we had to stop, and went round to what had been the back of the building to have a breather. The whole garden was full of corpses—there they all lay—men, women, children, and infants. Then, among the civilians standing in a dazed huddle, I noticed Marysia—miraculously, she was not even scratched. The scene made many of us who had never cried before, do so now—particularly because the dead were mostly women and children.

FRIDAY, SEPTEMBER 1

We hear that the Home Army Command has decided that it is no longer possible to hold the Old City, owing to lack of food and ammunition, and to enormous losses. Yesterday alone, three hundred soldiers of 'Chrobry I' Battalion died in a single sector of the Old City. So, the thin remnants of the Home Army garrison decided to escape through the sewers to the Center City. Their plan was as ambitious as it was radical.

It seems that at dawn the enemy attempted a surprise attack. This was repulsed, and some one hundred of the enemy were killed or wounded. However, at noon there came a simultaneous pincer attack—Ukrainian SS units from the Royal Castle Square and Germans from the north headed toward Krasiński Square. The famished and exhausted troops counterattacked with their last reserves of ammunition. Their devastating fire succeeded in keeping

An escape through the sewers

the attackers from entering Krasiński Square, where the manhole to freedom was located.

Leaving only token guards on the barricades, platoon after platoon, company after company, formed a long line. Then, with perfect discipline, the armed men descended one by one into the stinking, swift-flowing sewer.

The trip took four hours through waist-deep sludge and poisonous fumes. The human chain, each link holding tightly to the next one, snaked its way underground. Everyone had to move slowly, in total darkness and in silence. Those who slipped and fell in the deeper parts of the channels and had no strength to get up were drowned. The others could not spare precious time or reserves of energy to search for them, and without lights it was a hopeless task anyway.

SATURDAY, SEPTEMBER 2

As soon as the first rays of morning light fell upon the smoking ruins of the Old City, the *Stukas* began to dive-bomb Krasiński Square. Then, during the day, the enemy moved into the Old City, capturing some 35,000 civilians and 7,000 seriously wounded. Many of the wounded, lying in makeshift hospitals set up in the cellars below the ruins, were burned alive with flamethrowers. The old, disabled, sick, and all others unable to walk were lined up and shot, and the remainder were taken off to concentration camps.

SUNDAY, SEPTEMBER 3

Now that the Old City is taken, the enemy is trebling his attacks on our positions; the Germans want to finish us off, and as soon as possible.

So, in addition to employing heavy artillery, compressed air guns, missiles, and railway guns, the Germans have started mass air raids. *Stukas* fly low, relentlessly dropping bombs on Żoliborz.

At the same time, Praga—the Warsaw suburb on the other side of the Vistula—has been seized by the Red Army. One can see the Russian positions through field glasses.

The Old City

MONDAY, SEPTEMBER 4

We are now fighting in no-man's-land, the suburb of Marymont.

Early this morning, a group of drunken Ukrainian SS attacked our positions at the "Oil Mill" which has provided thousands of gallons of vegetable oil for our kitchens. Before the attack, we could hear the balalaikas playing as these Ukrainians danced the *kopak*. They also shot tracer bullets wildly into the sky, and the news reached us that they raped those women who were unlucky enough to get in their path.

At dawn, they began to storm the hill to the "Oil Mill." Staggering and shouting obscenities, they approached our positions. When they were well within range, we aimed a murderous fire at them. They withdrew in terror, leaving more than thirty bodies on the field.

Soon afterward, the German command sent a couple of captured Polish civilians to see Major 'Żubr,' Commander of the company whose units are defending the "Oil Mill." The Germans demanded that we allow them to collect the bodies of the fallen with the threat that, if the request were refused, they would execute ten Polish citizens for every dead Ukrainian. To prevent further mass murder of our civilians, we had no choice but to agree to their demands. We knew only too well that such threats are real.

WEDNESDAY, SEPTEMBER 6

Our detachment, together with the entire 229th Platoon, was sent today to take over and defend the Opel factory buildings. The extensive area of the plant, surrounded on all sides by a high masonry wall, borders on Słowacki Street on the east and the railroad tracks leading from the Warsaw–Gdańsk Station to Palmiry on the west. To the north, the area ends along Włościańska Street, and here the main gate to the compound, together with a small guardhouse, is located. To the south there are gardens, among the ruined fortifications of an old gunpowder factory.

I remember this place well, since during the early years of the Occupation I spent many a night there with a friend of mine exploring the underground labyrinths, searching for weapons and ammunition stored there by the Polish Army in September 1939. This was also the place which Ludwik had used for many a night meeting and for an arms cache, and it was near this factory wall that my friend and I attempted to disarm the German last year.

Adjoining the main building, which is the Assembly Hall, is a large, two-story brick extension. At the beginning of the Uprising the roof was only partly completed. It has no doors or windows, just rough openings, and I have dubbed it the "Brick-kiln." Next to it is a one-story building, and farther on is a tall structure with a wooden attic on the third floor. We have named this the High Hall, as it is the tallest building in the compound, and is located at one of the highest points in this part of Warsaw, so that from the attic we have the best possible view in all directions. Particularly strategic are the views north toward Bielany and west to Powązki, where the enemy's concentrations of artillery, armored cars, and tanks are located. From here we can also see what is happening eastward across the Vistula in Praga, where the Russian army is poised in immobilized silence.

As soon as we occupied the terrain, we began digging communication trenches at night. These trenches crisscross and connect all buildings and entrances to the compound, incorporating into our defense the makeshift bunkers which the Germans had hastily constructed before the onset of the Uprising.

It is an extremely difficult place to defend because the compound is situated in an open field, just about 600 meters from the enemy's guns, tanks, and infantry. In addition, the quarters of the German SS units in the Chemical Institute are less than two kilometers away, and the tanks of an SS *Panzer* Division are situated in the gardens.

When we seized the compound, we were taken by our commander to several key posts which we were supposed to cover particularly well because the enemy was so close to them. Cadet-Officer 'Konar's' detachment was given the job of defending the main gate of the compound. They quickly made themselves at home in the adjoining guardhouse and, since some Germans still did not realize that the Opel factory belonged to us now, visitors knocked at the big gate to be let in. Let in they were, and properly welcomed, too!

THURSDAY, SEPTEMBER 7

'Gazda,' 'Thur,' and I have been ordered to hold the "Brick-kiln." Some of the main observation posts are situated here. There is also a small gate leading into the gardens at this point—an important position, as it is very easy for the enemy to reach this place under cover of the trees. In the event that the enemy does break through, we are to attack and to engage him until the reinforcements arrive.

The second observation post, which is situated on the mezzanine floor, is as important as it is dangerous. The task of the observer is to watch the movements of the enemy through field-glasses and, if he notices anything unusual, he is to report it at once to the commander, using a field telephone mounted below the window opening.

One has to climb to this mezzanine floor by means of a Fire Brigade ladder because there are no stairs, and a careless movement of the head at this observation post can draw a burst from an enemy machine gun.

The task of the third observer is to keep an eye on the gardens from the ground. We change guards at these three points every three hours in order to keep awake, for we are on duty around the clock.

FRIDAY, SEPTEMBER 8

In the morning and evening, warm coffee and bread are brought to our posts by the nurses. Soup is brought in the middle of the day. We have a tough job, and the poor food and cold, sleepless nights are weakening us.

SATURDAY, SEPTEMBER 9

'Korwin' sometimes leaves the warmth and comfort of the bunker in the Health Center (and the company of our attractive front-line nurses) to inspect the posts. We object strongly to having our concentration broken by someone creeping up on us from behind, as we have enough to do watching for the enemy! So this evening, when 'Korwin' was within hearing range, the two of us on duty

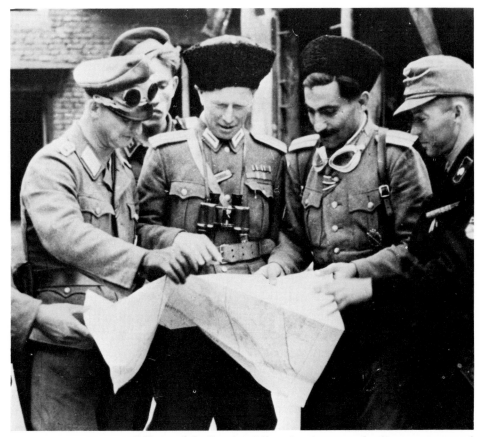

Officers of the Russian Liberation Army, under German command

clicked the safety catches on our rifles before shouting at him to stop and give the password. The noise reverberated against the walls of the empty, cavernous Assembly Hall. It stopped 'Korwin' in his tracks, and he whispered, "Don't shoot!"

MONDAY, SEPTEMBER 11

The last few days have been relatively quiet for us since only the open spaces of the compound are under fire from mortars and grenade-throwers. Żoliborz is still under very heavy artillery fire, but since the strong Russian antiaircraft guns across the river could now easily bring them down, *Stuka* dive-bombers can no longer bomb the city.

249

I have, however, just spent another long night's vigil in this lonely and dangerous place, and the need for constant vigilance even when we are not directly under attack, combined with the cold and hunger, make me feel very weary but very possessive about this pile of bricks which, with my comrades, I am defending.

THURSDAY, SEPTEMBER 14

News has reached us that Praga is still held by the Red Army, so the Germans are frantically rushing to block or destroy all bridges across the Vistula.

Our position has again attracted the enemy's attention, and today I noticed from my observation post gun muzzles pointing toward us. I had just enough time to slip down the ladder before the "Brick-kiln" was shaken by exploding shells. Even when we are under fire, we are not, of course, allowed to leave our observation posts, and so after each burst of shots I must return to my position.

At midday, they sent a *Stuka* to eliminate our observation post. It bore down, its machine guns firing directly at me, it seemed. It came so close that I could see the pilot's expression. The war suddenly seemed totally personal; then, with a thunderous roar the plane climbed steeply and was gone. The resulting silence shook me even more than the previous noise.

FRIDAY, SEPTEMBER 15

We are beginning to doubt the results of our efforts. Only the nights are free from artillery fire—except when the Germans fire at Soviet airplanes. These planes fly over our positions and drop us food and arms—but without parachutes, so that three-quarters of these supplies are smashed and useless. Still, the remainder is sufficient to keep us alive and fighting. That is good enough for Soviet purposes and for Soviet propaganda.

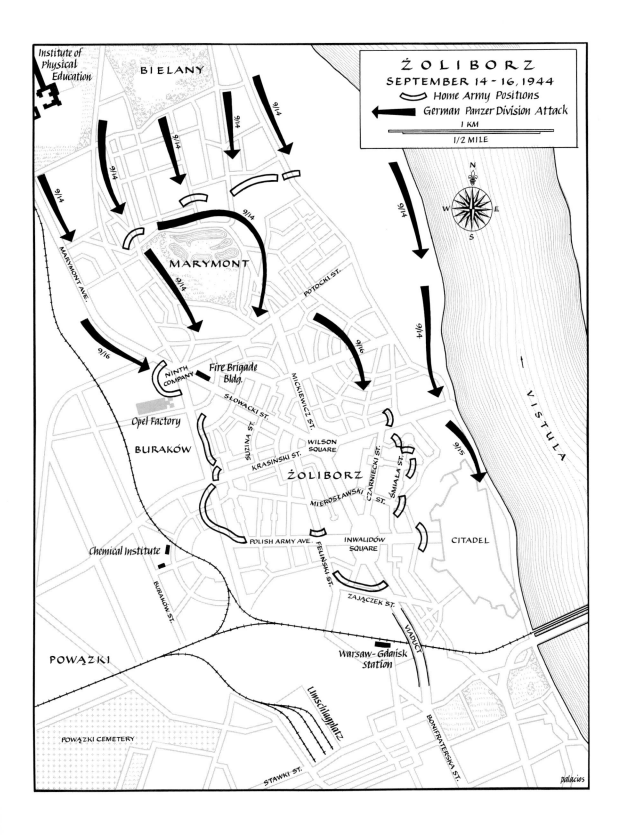

ŻOLIBORZ
SEPTEMBER 14 – 16, 1944
Home Army Positions
German Panzer Division Attack
1 KM
1/2 MILE

Institute of Physical Education

BIELANY

9/14
9/14
9/14
9/14
9/14
9/14
9/14

MARYMONT

MARYMONT AVE.

POTOCKI ST.

9/16
9/16

9/16

VISTULA

9/14

9/16

NINTH COMPANY

Fire Brigade Bldg.

Opel Factory

SŁOWACKI ST.

BURAKÓW

SUZINA ST.

MICKIEWICZ ST.

WILSON SQUARE

KRASIŃSKI ST.

ŻOLIBORZ

CZARNIECKI ST.

ŚMIAŁA ST.

MIEROSŁAWSKI ST.

CITADEL

Chemical Institute

POLISH ARMY AVE.

FELIŃSKI ST.

INWALIDÓW SQUARE

BURAKÓW ST.

ZAJĄCZEK ST.

POWĄZKI

VIADUCT

Warsaw-Gdańsk Station

Umschlagplatz

POWĄZKI CEMETERY

BONIFRATERSKA ST.

STAWKI ST.

palacios

SATURDAY, SEPTEMBER 16

At noon, as I was intently observing the area outside the compound wall, I noticed a couple of soldiers dragging a body to the shade of an apple tree, not 100 meters distant. I focused my field glasses upon them. They were a couple of Ukrainian SS men, and the body—dead or nearly dead—was that of a young girl. They placed her on the soft grass, spreading her legs wide. One of them waved his hand and four other soldiers emerged from behind the trees.

They encircled her and the first two at once started to take off their trousers. One of the Ukrainians mounted the body of the girl; the others crouched around watching. The girl did not struggle. While the first one finished, and before the second mounted the body, the girl's legs flopped limply. She was dead.

Our standing orders are not to fire until the enemy enters the side gate into the compound. But now, a shot suddenly rang out and the Ukrainian collapsed on the body of the girl. The others started running back toward their lines.

'Thur,' who was on duty with me, jumped up behind me to find out what was happening. I handed him my field glasses. I didn't say anything, but he understood.

SUNDAY, SEPTEMBER 17

It is now Sunday, and the rest of our Platoon—the 226th—has just joined us. It is really good to see my friends. We are to relieve the 229th Platoon, from which only 'Jocker' is to remain with us; he has a PIAT antitank gun.

Just as our platoon was taking over the compound, 'Jocker' was ordered to fire at one of the tanks on Włościańska Street. Accompanied by two soldiers carrying his missiles, he ran over to an opening in the wall, stuck the antitank gun through the hole, and pulled the trigger. The missile hit the tank on the other side of the wall.

I was on duty in the connecting trench between the Assembly Hall and the High Hall, and saw tanks breaking down the big gates and entering our compound, blazing away with their guns. 'Jocker' and his two men somersaulted into our trench. Shells from one of the tanks exploded nearby, seriously wounding 'Fugas,' who was still carrying on him the PIAT antitank missiles. Although he was immediately pulled out of the trench by his comrades, 'Fugas' died in their arms before they could reach the Health Center.

While the tanks were attacking, the enemy infantry took over the Assembly Hall and the fight continued between them and our men in the "Brick-kiln," through an opening in the common wall. The second missile fired from the PIAT by 'Jocker' was meant for the tanks, but it hit a pile of acetylene bottles nearby. As they began to explode, the tanks withdrew through the gate and hid behind the wall. Then the merciful night brought a much-needed respite.

MONDAY, SEPTEMBER 18

Today was a hot Indian summer day. After the cold nights, the midday sun warmed my tired bones as I sat on the scorched grass. How much longer?

Then I heard a new sound—a strong burring noise high in the sky. It quickly grew closer and more intense. A large flotilla of bombers was approaching. Flying in perfect military formation, the silver planes shimmered brilliantly in the sun. Around this formation of over one hundred Flying Fortresses of the U.S. Air Force, fighter planes were hovering protectively.

Suddenly, little black silhouettes appeared below the planes— the long-awaited Parachute Brigade? The parachutes now opened and began to float down slowly. The antiaircraft batteries opened up their full firepower, but most of the white shell explosions were not reaching high enough.

I could now see that the black shapes were not parachute troops, but long-promised supplies for us. Others, realizing this too, began to jump up and down with joy, embracing each other, clapping and shouting "Bravo." We now knew that our struggle was not as lonely as it had seemed during the last six weeks—that others would help in our hour of need.

TUESDAY, SEPTEMBER 19

The artillery bombardment has eased, but we are now constantly harassed by snipers. It is impossible to get to the High Hall or to the "Brick-kiln," as our trench is under constant fire from Ukrainian SS who are in the Assembly Hall. They are behind us, and the never-ceasing roar of the moving tanks meets our ears from the left and to the front. In addition, the grenade-throwers, mortars, and tanks have started to fire at our trench, the High Hall, and the "Brick-kiln."

We have been crouching in the bottom of the trench, pinned down and showered by pieces of exploding shells and grenades, but miraculously not suffering any losses. A little while ago, though, I suddenly felt that I was not in exactly the safest place. So, answering to my instincts, I moved about two meters to the right, and as soon as I left my previous position some quite large pieces of metal landed there. Providence certainly has an eye on me!

A little later, a corporal raised his head above the trench in order to see whether the tanks were moving in to attack us, and immediately a bullet from a Ukrainian rifle struck him. I opened his uniform and shirt, but I could see only the entrance hole in his back. The savages are shooting with dum-dum bullets!

As soon as night comes, we hope to withdraw under the cover of darkness to the High Hall and the Health Center.

WEDNESDAY, SEPTEMBER 20

Early this morning, we were again greeted by a mortar shell which fell in front of the makeshift bunker where 'Sławek' and 'Thur' were on duty. Part of the exploding shell flew into the bunker, hitting 'Thur' in the heart. The seventeen-year-old boy received two mortal wounds and died instantly, spurting blood onto his friend nearby. 'Sławek' fortunately was not wounded.

'Thur' had been on duty with me forty-eight hours before his death. We had talked to each other a lot, and 'Thur' had told me he had a feeling that he would be killed and was terribly sorry that he would not see his mother again. I told him it was nonsense. But he was right. His last wish was to be buried in the Żoliborz gardens, among the trees and flowers. He hated the idea of being buried beneath ruins.

THURSDAY, SEPTEMBER 21

'Thur's' wish has been carried out; today he was buried with military honors in a small cemetery in the middle of the gardens. Colonel 'Żywiciel,' Lieutenant 'Szeliga,' and a priest, along with our detachment, were at the burial ceremony.

Sidewalk burial, 1944 Uprising

Freedom Fighter's burial, 1944 Uprising

Sidewalk funeral, 1944 Uprising

MONDAY, SEPTEMBER 25

We have been directed to Wilson Square, where we are supposed to rest. We have been relieved at last by the other platoons of our company, and we are looking forward to the break, but my overtired condition has again brought on a high fever.

TUESDAY, SEPTEMBER 26

During a lull in the fighting, I stumbled along an unrecognizable street to a makeshift field hospital. A doctor there looked at me and sent me home to Feliński Street, where I went straight to bed.

WEDNESDAY, SEPTEMBER 27

My fever will not leave me. I feel very depressed because, while all my friends are fighting, I am flat in my bed. But I am so weak that I cannot even get up without help. The pain in my stomach, head, and chest has exhausted me completely. Marysia visited me yesterday afternoon—she had managed to get a pass from the hospital where she works. I was not fully conscious, so I remember only that she was there and that her soft, gentle voice was very soothing.

THURSDAY, SEPTEMBER 28

Early this morning, the Germans launched a strong attack from the direction of the Warsaw–Gdańsk Station. At nine o'clock they seized Prince Poniatowski School with the help of *Goliats*. The latter are small robot tanks filled with explosives and steered by remote control by cables or radio. Our house is separated from the school only by the width of Polish Army Avenue and two other houses, so I could see parts of the crumbling building from my bedroom window.

My father has also been lying ill with a fever at home. Aunt Stacha is our only mainstay, for the Germans have already taken Aunt Wanda and no one knows where she is. Mother is still at Baniocha, and the house is filled with strangers taking refuge there. My bedroom has been turned into a shambles because of a Soviet

Goliats (*German robot tanks*)

armsdrop without the benefit of a parachute, which hit the house last night.

My father's wounds from his escape through the sewers are not yet healed, and I, still weak, have a very high fever and am spitting blood. Father and I can not stay at home any longer, however, no matter how sick we are. So around noon we crawled from our beds, dressed ourselves as best we could, and left the house.

We went through the communication trenches, which were under artillery fire, and around Saint Stanisław Kostka Church to reach Wilson Square—or rather its ruins, since only piles of rubble marked many places where buildings had once stood.

In these surroundings, I said good-bye to my father, not knowing whether I would ever see him again.

I went to the building where our company had its headquarters, and a dreadful scene stretched before my eyes. Among the ruins of the Warsaw Cooperative Housing Colony, the grotesquely positioned corpses of women and children lay in bomb craters. Other bodies hung from the balconies. Even the once lush green trees of Żoliborz were now uprooted and entangled with the dead.

After some searching around the rubble and cellars, I finally found one of the nurses from our company. She took me to a cellar where there were already a few wounded people. 'Wilk' was among them, convalescing, along with another wounded Cadet-Officer and a beautiful young girl, a nurse who had been wounded in the legs. I spent the rest of the day there, under never-ceasing artillery fire.

FRIDAY, SEPTEMBER 29

The Germans are now advancing at a terrific speed. This evening they took over Saint Stanisław Kostka Church and gained ground along one side of Krasiński Street. From a window in our cellar, we could easily see the tanks rolling along the boulevard. Then, after taking positions in front of the apartment house we were holding, they began to destroy it methodically.

Because the enemy was so very near, we decided it would be better to rejoin our company, so we left the cellar under cover of darkness, crawling away over the sharp rubble on hands and knees.

Warsaw in flames

I noticed that I was not cold anymore. The whole of Żoliborz was on fire, and the flames illuminated the streets, warming the air around us.

All this time, the Red Army waited in silence in Praga, on the opposite side of the Vistula River, promising every day to send help and telling us to keep on fighting. Not a single company crossed the river.

Then the Germans attacked with full-sized tanks as well as *Goliats*. All communication between our units broke down, and each detachment was now completely on its own. By late afternoon, the Germans had driven deeply into the southern section of Żoliborz, toward Wilson Square and Krasiński Street. The artillery fire ceased only when night fell.

This evening we heard that General Bór-Komorowski had notified London that our situation is desperate, and that capitulation is inevitable unless large quantities of arms are received at once.

At the same time, he sent a message to Colonel 'Żywiciel' to keep on fighting, if only for one more day.

During the night I joined my friends, and helped them to defend our building against strong attacks by the enemy. I stood

Cross of Defiance

behind the window in the cellar bunker, so weak that I was hardly able to stay on my feet—let alone to continue firing—but now and then I would climb the ruins of the staircase and throw grenades upon the attacking Germans.

SATURDAY, SEPTEMBER 30

It is now Saturday. At nine o'clock this morning the enemy managed to set the second and third floors of our building on fire. We had to stand at our posts, deafened by exploding shells, our eyes smarting from the smoke.

It was so dark that none of us knew what was happening, and the groans of the wounded were making us more and more despondent. It was now clearly impossible to hold Żoliborz any longer, and shortly after ten o'clock Colonel 'Żywiciel' ordered the companies to withdraw in the direction of the Vistula. We were to cross the river at night and join the Russians.

Our company, which by that time was reduced to less than half its full strength, was again to be the last one to leave its position. The Commandos were always first to attack and last to leave. That was our job. However, at noon the order came from Lieutenant 'Szeliga,' and under cover of smoke we started to withdraw. Creeping through ruined houses, we reached a building on Mickiewicz Street. The remnants of our division gathered here while the Germans found themselves at last in possession of almost the whole of Żoliborz.

The rows of tanks standing on Wilson Square and lining Słowacki Street fired a stream of shells at us. The Germans had thrown an entire armored division into an area the size of a postage stamp. The Fire Brigade Building was blown to smithereens by an attack from *Goliat* robot tanks.

SATURDAY, SEPTEMBER 30   AFTERNOON

We had hoped to remain here until nightfall and then, after breaking through the German positions by the river, to reach the Russian boats that were supposed to be waiting for us.

261

German troops

The tanks were causing heavy damage, and I received an order to fire at them from my PIAT antitank missile thrower. It was now almost beyond my strength even to lift it; the fever had made me so weak that I was falling down every few meters. In order to ready the PIAT for action, I had to lie on my back to pull its spring.

I took a position in the ruins opposite a large Tiger tank, and my first missile hit the right tread of the tank, immobilizing it. I saw the huge gun slowly turning, finally pointing straight at me. I knew I had to get him this time. The second shell blew a large hole in the center, and flames shot from the tank. The hatch opened, and a black-uniformed crew started to jump out. The first man was cut down by our machine-gun fire. The second was killed as he was attempting to leave through the hatch. As he fell back, he grabbed the open hatch door, closing it. Nobody else left the steel trap.

My PIAT hit several tanks as we moved among the ruins. For once, there was an ample supply of missiles, and they were being handed to me one by one. Finally, I could no longer pull the spring and collapsed, utterly exhausted.

262

Polish fighters, 1944 Uprising

SATURDAY, SEPTEMBER 30   EVENING

When I came to, it was late evening. The enemy's fire had stopped, and there was only a stark and deathly silence. Its suddenness surprised and alarmed me greatly. What could it mean?

At this time we received an order to move through a communication trench to a building on the other side of the street. It was 34–36 Mickiewicz Street, the Glass House, and there the remainder of our Żoliborz Group had gathered.

When we reached the garden of the big building, we sat down on the grass and waited for further orders, warmed by the flames which surrounded the whole area.

While sitting there on the grass, I reminded myself how not that long ago I had spent such happy times here, visiting Marysia.

The stairs leading to the apartment where Marysia lived were not touched by fire, and in a daze from my fever I went up, but the rooms were badly damaged—broken furniture, window frames, and glass lying all over the floor.

263

The holes in the walls and roof made an awful impression on me and the thought nagged at my mind, Where is Marysia now? Is she still alive?

I lurched back down the stairs like a lunatic and met my startled companions. One of them shouted, "What the hell are you doing wandering around these ruins? Are you mad?"

I sank down on the steps near my fellow soldiers. The whole situation looked quite hopeless. We had to face a fact we had always known—had always known, even if not admitting it—that at some time we would have to be prepared for capture or death.

SATURDAY, SEPTEMBER 30 NIGHT

The news came through, striking like lightning. The message was starkly brief. Surrender! The word itself brought forth a furious barrage of oaths from all sides: "Lies!" "Impossible!" Still, all the companies were ordered to line up. We did so, not yet able to believe what was happening.

Lieutenant 'Szeliga' stood before our company. I had to struggle to stand to attention and to concentrate as he took a paper from his breastpocket and began to read aloud the order from Colonel 'Żywiciel':

> Soldiers!
>
> I thank you, my dear comrades, for everything you have accomplished during these two months of fighting with the enemy, for your efforts, pain, and courage.
>
> I am proud that I had the honor to command such soldiers as you.
>
> Remain such in the future and show the world what a Polish soldier is, he who will sacrifice everything for his country.
>
> Soldiers!
>
> An hour ago, as ordered by the Supreme Commander of the Armed Forces, General Bór-Komorowski, I signed the surrender document of our group. . . .

We are surrendering to the *Wehrmacht* as a regular army, and we will be treated according to the Geneva Convention.

I thank you once more for everything.
God be with you!

SATURDAY, SEPTEMBER 30   MIDNIGHT

After that, everything went like a nightmarish dream. Hardly realizing it, we began to fall into military formation. It was nearly midnight as we started our slow march uphill from the Glass House
along Mickiewicz Street toward Wilson Square.

We all made one last effort and marched in an even, measured
step, as on parade, our rifles on our shoulders. We had to remind
the Germans what kind of soldiers they had been fighting during
the last two months.

With officers at our flanks, we advanced toward Wilson
Square, solidly lined with tanks, where the Germans were waiting
for us. When we were about ten meters from a gate leading into the
courtyard of a large building, the command came: "*Kompania
Stój!*" (Company Halt!). Our commander exchanged words in German with the officer-in-charge. Then we entered the courtyard.

A thrill of terror shook me as I saw the faces and uniforms of
the hated enemy at such close range. The Germans at once surrounded us and confiscated our short arms, field glasses, and so on.
Then we marched in company formation through the courtyard;
passing the tanks standing at the entrance to Słowacki Street, we
found ourselves in the middle of Wilson Square, illuminated by the
flames of burning Żoliborz. Here, we had to lay down the rest of
our weapons.

I had nothing left to give up.

SUNDAY, OCTOBER 1

The Germans separated us into two parties—one consisting of Officers and Cadet-Officers, and the other of noncommissioned officers and the ranks. They then took us through the ruins and ashes

The anchor sign of Fighting Poland
(PW: Polska Walcząca)

of once-beautiful Żoliborz in the direction of Powązki Cemetery. At Powązki, the Germans put us in some military stables and shut us up for the night.

MONDAY, OCTOBER 2

At ten o'clock in the morning, a carload of leather-coated Gestapo men arrived. Unable to touch us since we were under the "guardianship" of the SS Lower Saxony *Panzer* Division, they had to be satisfied with the mere sight of us. We looked at each other like savage animals. As it turned out, this was my last sight of the Gestapo. Fever tremors shook my body, and before my mind's eye passed Czarniecki Street; Pawiak; Szucha Avenue; Krasiński, Słowacki, Żeromski, Suzina, and a kaleidoscope of other familiar places that had become the battle stations and boulevards of war.

At noon, trucks took us to a camp in Pruszków, near Warsaw. On the way we passed the Jewish Cemetery bordering the burned-out remains of the Ghetto.

My fever was rapidly worsening, and I now had a racking cough. Hardly able to move, I shamelessly prayed for a quick end; but it was not to be—this was only another beginning.

At Pruszków we were put into a cold dank hall, but because I was so ill I was moved into a smaller room, where the officers looked after me. I was hardly aware of what was happening.

266

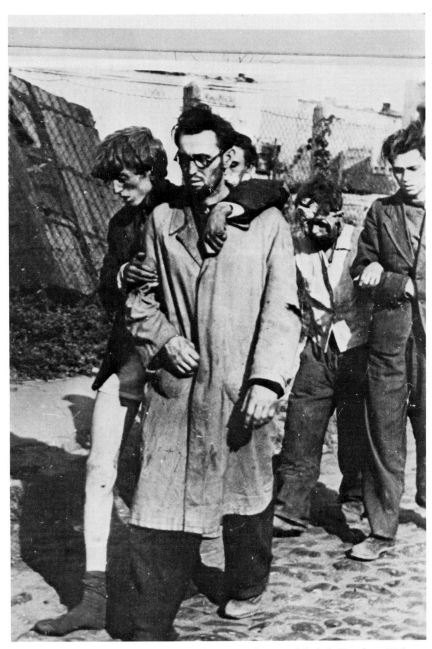

Captured Polish Freedom Fighters

267

The march to captivity

The cattle train

THURSDAY, OCTOBER 5 MORNING

Some of our troops from the Center City were brought to Pruszków this morning, and it seems that our capitulation is now complete. They had brought with them a few copies of the last Home Army *Information Bulletin*, and one of our officers came to wake me up so that he could read it to me:

> Home Army *Information Bulletin*
> October 4, 1944
> Last Number (102/310)

> The battle is over . . . but the defeat is the defeat of one city, of one stage in our fight for freedom. It is not the defeat of our Nation, of our plans and historical ideals. From the spilled blood, the common hardship and difficulties, from the suffering of bodies and of souls, there will rise a new Poland—free, strong, and great.
> With this faith we will live in forced, homeless wanderings or in prison camps, just as we live with it in our work and battles. This faith is the most real, the highest testament written with the blood of the many thousands of victims and heroes of the Uprising.

THURSDAY, OCTOBER 5 AFTERNOON

Late in the afternoon of the fourth day we were herded like animals to a cattle train, probably one of those that had been used to take so many to Auschwitz, Majdanek, and Treblinka. Sixty of us were to be allotted to each car. The fine cold drizzle of late autumn reinforced the melancholy I could not put aside, and I was shivering continuously by now.

Before the train set off we were addressed by the escort commander of the same Lower Saxony *Panzer* Division we had fought against in Żoliborz. Standing on the steps of the train in his black battledress, the commander congratulated us on our bravery and on the strong resistance we had put up. He said he was proud that his division had had the chance to fight against such courageous soldiers. After he left, we were all pushed on board, and the train drew slowly out of the station.

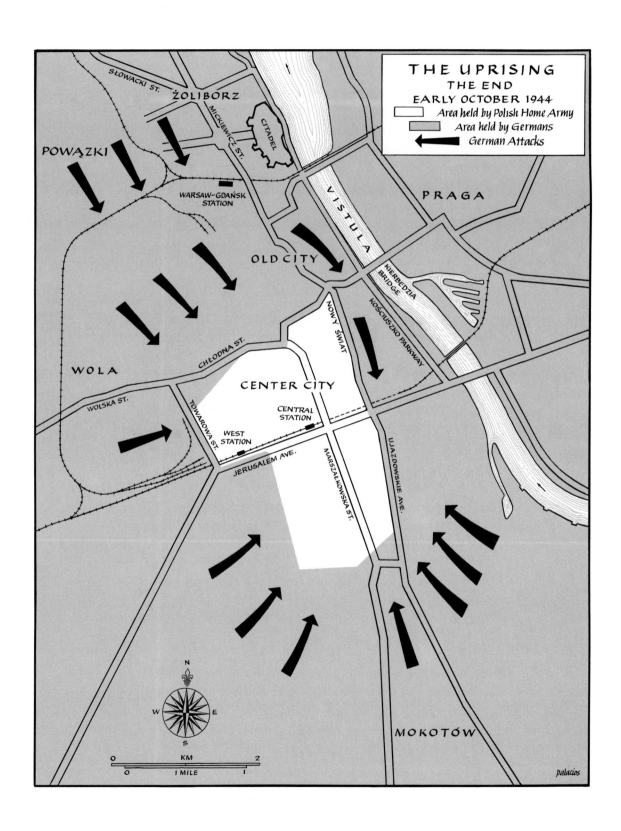

THE UPRISING
THE END
EARLY OCTOBER 1944

Area held by Polish Home Army
Area held by Germans
German Attacks

SŁOWACKI ST.

ŻOLIBORZ

MICKIEWICZ ST.

CITADEL

POWĄZKI

WARSAW-GDAŃSK
STATION

VISTULA

PRAGA

OLD CITY

KIERBEDZIA
BRIDGE

NOWY ŚWIAT

KOŚCIUSZKO PARKWAY

CHŁODNA ST.

WOLA

CENTER CITY

WOLSKA ST.

TOWAROWA ST.

CENTRAL
STATION

WEST
STATION

ULAZDOWSKIE AVE.

JERUSALEM AVE.

MARSZAŁKOWSKA ST.

MOKOTÓW

N
W   E
S

0   KM   2
0   1 MILE   1

palacios

THURSDAY, OCTOBER 5 EVENING

The journey was unbearable. After we had been crammed into the wooden cattle wagon, the heavy sliding panels on one side were drawn shut and locked from the outside. We were in darkness, relieved only by a faint patch of light which filtered through a small, barred opening on one wall.

There wasn't enough room for all of us to sit down at once, and, in any case, the wooden planks which formed the floor of the wagon were extremely hard, cold, and uncomfortable.

Still weak from fever, I couldn't stand up by myself and, as the train rattled and jolted its way over the tracks, I kept falling onto my colleagues. They kindly made enough room for me so that I could sit down with my back against the side of the wagon.

Some time that night, the train shuddered to a halt, and we heard noises and talking outside. Then there was a clang as the side panel was unbolted from outside, and scraping as it was pulled open a few inches. Finally, an armed German guard pushed some jugs of coffee and some hardtack biscuits through the opening. In answer to our many questions, he told us only that we were at a place called Skierniewice and that the food had been requisitioned for us from the civilian population there. Then he said we'd better hurry up and finish, as we'd soon be moving on again. The door closed. I tried to eat, but couldn't, and barely sipped the coffee.

Sure enough, a little while later the bolt clanged fast, and we set off again.

The break and the refreshments seemed to stimulate us out of the daze into which most of us had fallen when we were first pushed into the train. I did not join in the chatter, and didn't even really want to listen; I just wanted to sit there by myself, with my own thoughts and fears. But I couldn't help hearing snatches of the conversation—the speculation as to our destination, how long we might be there, and so on. No one dared bring up the question of what might be happening to our comrades and families back in Warsaw, but inevitably the talk turned to that of escape.

We knew the train was heavily guarded, and the *Panzer* commander's farewell speech—full of praise as it was for our courageous fighting—had made it clear that anyone trying to escape would be shot immediately.

271

All we knew was that we would not be going to a civilian camp like Auschwitz, but that we would be heading west—probably into Germany itself—to a military camp.

The talking soon stopped, however, and the wagon became quiet again as we all fell into uneasy, fitful sleep.

FRIDAY, OCTOBER 6

As a weak ray of daylight entered through the barred opening, people woke up and tried to stretch their cramped, stiff limbs. But I couldn't find the energy to move, and remained huddled against the side of the wagon. Some of my companions took turns at watching from the window to see what towns we passed through and tried to guess where we might be heading. When the train did pass through an inhabited place, our red and white armbands were defiantly waved from the window.

Aside from the crowding and the discomfort, the fear and the hunger, another humiliating aspect of our journey into captivity had to be faced. Since we had now been in the wagon for more than twelve hours and had not been able to get out, even when we stopped at Skierniewice, we had to relieve ourselves in one corner of the wagon. The stench soon became overpowering. That cattle car was a Pawiak on wheels.

I must confess I was so sick that I hardly knew, or cared, what was going on around me. Once in a while, though, one of my companions would sit beside me and try to cheer me up with conversation. I was by far the youngest of the soldiers in our wagon, and had been separated from most of my company, so that I was really very lonely.

Toward evening, the train began a series of shunting maneuvers, and those watching from the window said that we appeared to be pulling off the main line onto a side track. They speculated that this had been done to let a military train pass through. There must have been quite heavy military traffic, for we sat there for several hours.

As night fell, we assumed that we would move on, but suddenly we heard the wail of an air-raid siren and some time later we heard bomb explosions and antiaircraft fire. We cheered, for this meant that the Allies were overhead on a bombing raid! It also meant, of course, that we had stopped in a major city, probably Berlin, and that we were thus already deep into enemy territory—Germany.

At this thought, we soon became subdued, and the proximity of the bombing exaggerated our helplessness and fear. Fortunately, we were not hit, but from the commotion outside the Germans must have been getting it badly.

SATURDAY, OCTOBER 7

Early in the morning the train lurched off again, and another day of hunger and discomfort began. I just lay there, ill enough by now that I couldn't even talk.

SUNDAY, OCTOBER 8

My friends woke me up early this morning to say that we were leaving the train—whatever our destination was, we had reached it. When the side panel of the wagon was finally dragged open, the morning light seemed blinding after the days of darkness, but the fresh air was unbelievably welcome. As we got off the train, in a fine drizzle under cloudy skies, my first impression was of an evergreen forest stretching as far as I could see. I also saw that the station had a name board—Alten Grabow—but the name meant nothing to me.

The Germans then formed us into groups and marched us a kilometer or so to an enormous wire-enclosed camp, with huge double gates. I didn't exactly march, but stumbled along with the help of a couple of my friends.

We waited in the rain, while they apparently decided what to do with us. I asked someone where our officers were, and another man (who spoke fluent German) said he had heard the Germans referring to another camp being reserved for officers. He also said that the barracks in this camp—Stalag 11-A—were full, and that we would have to sleep in tents. Sure enough, a little later we were put to work erecting huge marqueelike tents on the open ground

The camp

between the barracks and the perimeter fence. About 150 men were assigned to each.

We had no bedding of any kind, of course, so had to sleep on the bare ground—although even this was comfortable after the wooden floor of the cattle car.

That night, however, it poured with rain, and we had to get up and dig channels around the tent to let the water run away. The next morning, I was again so weak I couldn't get up, and that meant I couldn't eat, for you only got food if you went and stood in the line near the kitchen yourself. By this time, I really didn't care, and just lay on the wet ground wishing it would all end. My friends would sneak food over to me whenever they could, although, if caught, they would have been shot.

I spent several days this way, until a friend of mine who spoke English fetched a British camp medic to look at me. Until then, I had not realized that Stalag 11-A housed prisoners of war of many nationalities. I also found out it was a big camp, containing tens of thousands of men. In spite of its size, however, the administration of the camp was most efficient. The Germans kept detailed records of each prisoner, and I soon received my camp number— prisoner-of-war number 45517.

The medic finally returned and said he had managed to arrange for me to be sent to the camp hospital, along with several of my colleagues who were also sick. But, he warned me, the hospital was almost three kilometers away, and I would have to go there on foot.

SATURDAY, OCTOBER 14

I do not know how long it took us to reach that hospital, or how we got there at all, in fact. As did many of the others, I lurched along like a drunken old man, falling down frequently and convinced each time that I would never get up again. But somehow we made it to the Gross Lübars *Lazarett*.

SUNDAY, OCTOBER 15

The hospital consisted of flimsily built wooden barracks, with board beds. The barracks for Polish troops were already filled to capacity with wounded, but finally they found room for us in one of the Italian barracks. The room was filthy, and the beds were infested with bugs from the dirty straw mattresses. Still, it was somewhere to lie down other than the ground, and we did at least have a flimsy blanket apiece.

I was burning up one minute and shivering the next, and now when I coughed I brought up flecks of blood. Many of the other men in the ward were in the same condition. Ironically, we had to converse with the Italians in broken German, the only language we had in common. I discovered that there were no nurses assigned to the *Lazarett*, although a doctor came to do his "rounds" each morning. In fact, we were in isolation, with each barrack enclosed by a wire fence and out-of-bounds to the others.

Sure enough, next morning a doctor arrived and carefully examined each of us in turn. In my case, he solemnly advised lots of bed rest and good food as the best cure for my illness. What a farce, for the painful pangs of hunger never left us for an instant!

SUNDAY, OCTOBER 22

The days passed very slowly, and we became more and more apathetic. The food was just sufficient to keep us alive.

In the morning at seven o'clock, we got half a liter of dreadfully bitter liquid, neither coffee nor tea. At twelve o'clock we got three-quarters of a liter of turnip soup without any salt, fat, or potatoes in it; finally, in the evening we were given a piece of black bread weighing about thirty grams and a spoonful of red-beet jam. This scanty diet and my illness kept me in bed.

WEDNESDAY, NOVEMBER 1

Time drags by, and it's sometimes hard to separate one day from the next. I lie on my bed, weaker than ever, and thoroughly convinced I will not get out of here alive. My physical weakness is by now no greater than my mental depression.

FRIDAY, NOVEMBER 3

My spirits have improved, for today some of the nurses from our battalion found out where I was and came over to see me. I am particularly pleased to find that the twins, Barbara and Danuta, are among them. They are working in the camp kitchen. Now that they know where I am, they say that they can take care of me and will try to bring me additional rations whenever they can. Just seeing them and being able to talk to them is wonderful, of course, because no one except the doctor ever comes here.

SATURDAY, NOVEMBER 4

Every day, it seems, someone dies. There is no one to take the bodies away, though, so we just have to cover their faces with a blanket and wait until the doctor comes again. He then arranges for prisoner orderlies to come and remove the bodies. Nobody says where they are taken, and we can't bring ourselves to ask.

The beds don't stay empty for long; the dead are soon replaced with the sick or the wounded.

SUNDAY, NOVEMBER 5

Today is very special. I have written my first letter to the family. The Germans have special paper even for this—a two-part letter form specially printed for military prisoners of war. The prisoner writes on the first part of the form, leaving the second portion blank for the reply, and then the whole thing folds up into a sort of self-made envelope. I can't be too open in what I say, of course, because we know that the letters have to pass the camp censor.

I know there is no use writing to anyone at Feliński Street, for I'm sure that the house isn't even standing now, let alone with anyone living there. God knows where Father is—probably in a camp somewhere, if he's still alive—so I have written to Mother at Baniocha. I presume she is there with my sister.

5 November 1944

Dear Mother:

I am healthy, in one piece, and in a prisoner-of-war camp. The last time I saw Father and Aunt Stacha was more than a month ago at home on Feliński Street. Everybody in the house was in one piece and healthy. Since then I have had no news. Writing this letter I am uncertain whether it will reach its destination, but maybe God will let it. Maybe it will reach you before your Name's Day, bringing you my greetings and kisses. How are you, Wanda, and everybody? I can imagine what you must have lived through, not having had any news from us for so long. That is why I want so much for this letter to reach you. If it does, please write to me what is happening at home and give me the names of relatives I have in Cracow or the Reich, so that I could send them my food package vouchers. Maybe Aunt Petecka or Uncle in Silesia.

I spent August and September in Zoliborz. I have written to the Red Cross for news of Aunt Stacha and Father. I hope that all of us, with God's help, will find each other.

Kisses,
Julek

I pray that the letter reaches them somehow, for then they will know that I am still alive and will know where I am.

WEDNESDAY, NOVEMBER 15

Another pleasant surprise today—we have received some more Red Cross parcels. The first ones came about the end of October, but each one had to be shared among sixteen men, so we got no more than a spoonful of jam or powdered milk each. Now, however, each parcel only has to be shared among four men. They are still so small, however, that we ate everything at once and will be hungry again tomorrow. Still, these parcels cheer us up no end, as does the sound of Allied bombers going over the camp at night on their way deep into Germany. Our only fear is that one day the Allies may have to decide to drop bombs on our camp, for rumor has it that there is a big underground munitions factory at Alten Grabow; thus the camp is not just a place to keep prisoners, it is also a camouflage and protective cover for arms production.

MONDAY, NOVEMBER 20

More and more wounded prisoners of various nationalities keep coming into the hospital. But most of them have not been wounded in battle—they come here to recover from injuries received while doing forced labor in the nearby mines and stone quarries. Some of them have been beaten for not working hard enough to suit the German guards.

TUESDAY, NOVEMBER 21

One of these wounded men came over to talk to me today. A Scot, he had met other Poles when our army was in training in Scotland, and he wanted to tell me about his home. He carried some dog-eared photographs of his family, which he proudly showed to me several times.

Conversing in a pidgin mixture of English, Polish, and German, he told me that prisoners from the main camp who were used for forced labor had to work up to twelve hours a day, even though they, too, only got starvation-level rations. Two weeks of this was usually enough to weaken them utterly, and many were injured; the guards beat the rest for not working fast enough. Wounded and beaten alike, they were sent to the *Lazarett*, where most of them died.

THURSDAY, NOVEMBER 23

I tried to find my Scottish friend today, since he didn't pay me another visit yesterday evening. I was told he died yesterday morning from the beating he had received at the mine. I feel very depressed again. The days and nights drag by, marked only by our scanty meals and the play-acting of the doctor's visits. I still have had no reply from my family, and my only prospect seems to be to die a slow death, at best in a hospital somewhere.

SATURDAY, NOVEMBER 25

The Italian prisoners, some of whom are actually officers, have been trying to cheer me up by teaching me Italian, and they have encouraged me to get up each day instead of lying there like a sad lump. I particularly like a song I have learned from them, but today the padre came over and asked me not to sing it out loud as the words were really rather dirty!

TUESDAY, NOVEMBER 28

Although the *Lazarett* is officially out-of-bounds, other prisoners have started to come and visit us. Maybe the twins have told them how lonely we are. They cheer us up and give us plenty to talk about later by telling us stories of the different nationalities in the camp. Each contingent reacts differently to camp life, it seems.

The British are friendly but rather shy and reserved. They play football a lot. The Sikhs and Ghurkas who come to visit us have been trying to teach me how to play whist, and I've been teaching them Polish.

The Dutch seem to be friends with everybody, but like the rest of the prisoners, they ignore the French, who have talked their way out of forced labor by openly going along with the Germans.

The colonial troops and the Americans are the only non-European soldiers here.

Funny as these stories are, funniest of all are our efforts to communicate with each other in pidgin mixtures of various languages mixed with mime and little sketches on scraps of paper.

WEDNESDAY, NOVEMBER 29

I felt so much better today that I decided to walk over to the camp kitchen to see the twins. Surprisingly, nobody stopped me as I left the hospital, but I soon realized how weak I still was, for I began to feel dizzy before I had gone halfway. I had to sit and rest for quite a while before I felt well enough to make the return trip, and even then one of the girls walked with me.

FRIDAY, DECEMBER 1

Today the world seems brighter altogether. I have received a letter written by my father. My letter to Mother had arrived on November 15—two days after her Name's Day. They had received verbal news of me on November 13 itself, from the father of a friend of mine here. His letter had reached his family before mine got through, so unfortunately my parents knew I was sick. I had carefully not mentioned this in my letter to them! After inquiring anxiously about my health, Father gave me news of the family:

16 November 1944

Dear Julek:

We were thrilled with the news about you, received first from Mr. Hoppe and then two days later your letter arrived. Next time give us news of your state of health in detail because we are worried. We are all here together and healthy, Mother with Wanda,

Aunt Stacha, the Kipas and I. Write at once to Uncle
Władek and Uncle Stefan, whose address is Gródziec
near Bendsburg 65, Grubenstrasse 1. Are you receiv-
ing packages yet? Grandma Hala is also at Baniocha,
Aunt Wanda and Mary are probably in Germany; no
news of Aunt Zosia and her husband. In Komorów
(Klonowa 16) I saw the Chojnackis, but no news of
Lolek and his wife. Don't you need warm clothing?
The first news of you came on Mother's Name's Day.
We all embrace you warmly and send greetings, be-
lieving that we will see you soon.

Parents

TUESDAY, DECEMBER 5

Barbara and Danuta came over today and brought news of Marysia; she is living with her mother in a small town in central Poland. I
wrote a long letter to her at once, but do not know if it will ever
reach her. I have also written to my Uncle Władek and Aunt Tosia
in London. Finally, I heard that poor old Aunt Wanda and Mrs.
Bernardyńska (my history teacher) are both in Ravensbrück.

FRIDAY, DECEMBER 15

It is very cold now. Fortunately, the latest Red Cross parcels from
Britain contained clothing as well as food. I now have a warm battledress uniform, a sweater, and a proper blanket. The twins are sew-
ing a little homemade Polish flag on my forage cap for me, and I'm
still using the military boots that I was wearing at the time of the
surrender. But I wonder how much longer they'll have to do? Still,
what a luxury it is to have some clean clothes—maybe for a while
we'll get a break from picking lice off ourselves.

Our washing facilities still consist of only two cold water taps,
so we're not the cleanest or freshest of people these days. Fortunately, we're all equally grubby and stale, so that only our visitors
are really put off!

SATURDAY, DECEMBER 23

Christmas is coming and we have been saving food for a Christman Eve dinner we planned to share with the girls. But today, just two days before Christmas, the Germans have taken them away to another camp.

Beaten and herded together by the Germans, the girls had to wait in the frost and snow for a train which took them to a special camp for women from the Home Army. Some of them were seriously wounded and were left lying on stretchers in the snow for several hours. In spite of all that we had seen and been through, this still struck us as unbelievably cruel.

Their departure is very painful to describe. Even some of the older, seasoned soldiers wept while saying good-bye to them. After they had gone away, there was silence and everyone realized just how much they had done for us, and how much they meant to us. At the same time I can't help being glad that we still have such feelings left—that the Germans haven't succeeded in demoralizing us to the extent that we are impervious to suffering.

SUNDAY, DECEMBER 24

So, I am spending Christmas Eve with my memories, thinking of the table around which my family will be sitting for the traditional dinner, and wondering which of us will live. I know there will already be empty chairs at the table for Uncle Norbert, for me, and for Aunt Wanda.

MONDAY, DECEMBER 25   CHRISTMAS DAY

The Dutch contingent staged an amateur play and talent show today, and invited us over in an effort to cheer us up. But it is hard not to be despondent—I was not even able to say good-bye to the twins, and it seems that I have lost my last link with home. I have had two more letters from my parents, but nothing has changed there and there's only so much they can say in one page anyway.

282

1945

MONDAY, JANUARY 1

The New Year. The Belgians marked the occasion by putting on a play, and it helped take our minds off the war for a while. It also helped me stop thinking about my stomach, which was in revolt after I had greedily gobbled my Christmas food package all at one go.

My frequent trips to the latrine were not only unpleasant but very embarrassing. And now I have another problem. Surprisingly, the Germans did not confiscate our few remaining personal possessions when we came to the camp, and I had on me at the time a bundle of worthless old *złoty* bills, which ever since I have been using as toilet paper. Now I am rapidly running out!

WEDNESDAY, JANUARY 3

As the Red Army has occupied the rest of Poland, I am now getting no letters from home at all. Also, the camp is getting more and more overcrowded, but the news the incoming prisoners bring is good. The Allies are getting closer and closer, which makes the guards more and more nervous. We have begun to tease them, joking that they would be better off joining us as prisoners rather than waiting for the Russians. I guess even the Germans are now admitting that they have lost the war.

WEDNESDAY, JANUARY 10

My health has really begun to improve now, in spite of everything, and the doctor has told me I will soon be able to leave the hospital. However, I have to pretend that I am still quite ill, as I know what it would mean to be sent to the main camp now and be subject to forced labor.

MONDAY, JANUARY 15

For some reason, the Germans have decided to demolish our *Lazarett* and all the patients, myself included, have been moved to another hospital in Alten Grabow. The barracks here are much better, but the food is the same everywhere.

Lazarett (*prisoner-of-war hospital*)

An American prisoner of war in Lazarett,
with Red Cross package

SATURDAY, JANUARY 20

I managed to pretend continued illness until Monday, but finally I am back in the main camp. About four hundred prisoners from the Home Army are housed in one barrack, and there is almost no room whatsoever. There are no real bunks, and we have to sleep on planks placed a foot above the stone floor, from which the dampness penetrates our bodies. There is no heat, and moisture streams down the walls even on dry days.

In such conditions and with no real washing or laundry facilities available, vermin are found everywhere. Like the others, I am infested with lice, and I have an itchy rash all over my body.

Knowing what it will mean if I am sent to work, I have discussed it with my comrades. They suggested I tell the camp officials that on leaving the hospital I was classified as "D.U." (unable to work), although actually the German doctor had told me otherwise. Because of the great disorder in the camp office now, I have succeeded in my plan, and today I was told that I am to be sent back to the hospital section. My comrades are pleased for my sake, but I am sorry I have to leave them.

British prisoners of war ("Tommies")

SUNDAY, JANUARY 28

Although my fever has gone and my lungs are better, I was not faking it completely when I claimed to be too sick to work. In addition to the incredibly itchy skin rash, which has now spread over my entire body, I am now having great difficulty in eating anything but soup and other liquids. My gums have receded, and my teeth are so loose I'm afraid they are going to fall out any day. Certainly I can't chew the claylike substance they give us in the name of bread, at least without soaking it thoroughly first.

TUESDAY, FEBRUARY 6

Although mail to and from Poland has stopped, things still get through from the *Reich*, and today I received a food parcel from my Uncle Stefan. He lives in a part of Silesia that belonged to Poland before it was annexed into the Third Reich in September 1939. I opened the package in great anticipation, my mouth watering. I pulled off the final paper, and there it was—a beautiful fat sausage, but covered completely in white and green mold!

My disappointment was so great that I rushed outside and threw the smelly mess over the fence. To my disgust, three Russian orderlies who were passing immediately made a grab at it and fought each other like dogs, tearing off huge chunks and gulping it down. My stomach churned, and I made a rush for the latrine.

WEDNESDAY, FEBRUARY 21

We are beginning to have some hope, as the news reaching us is very good. We have been told about the fighting on the Rhine and close to Berlin. The news becomes better every day, and the new American and Italian prisoners coming to our camp predict a quick finish. The bombardment of Germany has not stopped for the last six months and each week is becoming stronger. In neighboring Magdeburg, not one house is left standing after the RAF raids. Good for them. It avenges London, Warsaw, and other cities!

As the end approaches, our treatment has altered greatly, and now that the American Army has stopped behind the Elbe, our guards are trying to make friends with us.

Because a transport of wounded Russians has arrived, they have had to remove us from the hospital to make room for them, and have sent us back to the stables of Alten Grabow, which are a nightmare to us. As the stables are also full, they have put us on the bare floors of the lofts. I have a place just under a hole in the roof, through which—when it rains—a stream pours on me, waking me up. But now, with the hope of a speedy finish to all this, it is much easier for us to stand the cold and starvation.

Even the food situation has begun to improve since, in exchange for a few cigarettes, one can get out of the camp and trade —again with cigarettes—in the village.

Of course, all these proceedings are strictly unofficial, but in the village, in exchange for cigarettes, one can get such products as potatoes, beans, and sugar. We are not getting any more bread in our daily ration, but they have started to give us the horrible biscuits called *Knochenbrot*.

We spend our time listening to the roar of the front artillery and in talking to our German guards. We keep telling them that they will be much better off when *they* are *our* prisoners!

SATURDAY, MARCH 3

My sixteenth birthday, and the best present I could have received was the distant, but now constant, noise of the artillery as the Americans advanced.

SUNDAY, APRIL 1

By late March we were finally beginning to have real hope, especially when we heard that the Americans had reached the Elbe. Some even said that Germany had actually surrendered, but that was not true. Somehow, the waiting now is more demoralizing than ever; our liberation is now a real possibility, and yet we have no idea of how soon it will be.

Liberation Day at a prisoner-of-war camp in Germany

SATURDAY, APRIL 14

The German guards are now so anxious to make friends with us that they scarcely need to be bribed to let us leave the camp in order to go down to the village. Just one pack of cigarettes will do it. I stopped at the first house I came to, and a middle-aged German woman came to the door. Another pack of cigarettes got me a loaf of bread, then seeing my battledress, she asked if I was British. When I told her I was Polish and from Warsaw, she cried, "Oh, my God, you killed my son!" and slammed the door in my face.

Suddenly losing my nerve but holding firmly onto my precious loaf of bread, I made my way back to the camp as fast as I could.

SATURDAY, MAY 5

Then came the Third of May, the Polish national holiday, so a day which, even under these circumstances, was a special one for me. This Third of May became more special than all the rest.

American Red Cross trucks arrived at the camp in the morning to collect the American, British, Belgian, and Dutch prisoners of war. All the other nationalities were supposed to remain in the camp and wait for liberation by the Red Army. When I saw the uniforms of the American soldiers and officers, who threw some food

Flight to Freedom

and cigarettes over the wires to us, I tried to get out of the camp; but the gates were still closed and beside them stood German guards and members of the intracamp police—made up of all nationalities. They had orders to keep us in the camp until the final liberation.

As I stood behind the gate, there was so much chaos and crowding that I succeeded in slipping out under the arm of one of the policemen and made my way over to the trucks and the Americans.

After two hours of watching the trucks being filled with American and British soldiers, I suddenly had a great urge to go with them. It would be a tremendous risk as they had told us we were to be taken out the next day and, by leaving the camp, I would be without friends and at the mercy of strangers.

Yet, after so many days, months, and years, I was so starved for freedom that I decided to chance it. Truck after truck, marked with large white stars, started to leave the camp, cheered on by those staying behind. As I was looking around, I saw an American whom I knew from the camp sitting in one of the trucks. He knew a few sentences of broken Polish, and I had made friends with him. He noticed me and signaled to me to jump onto the moving truck. I did not wait any longer but in a second had climbed up, helped by the strong, kindly hands of the Yanks. My whole future, my fight, and my search for freedom now depended on that decision.

As the truck pulled away and gained speed, I waved my cap to my friends and companions, who were still standing behind the wire fence of the camp. Thus, two months to the day after my sixteenth birthday, I left Stalag 11-A and the bondage of the Third Reich.

Epilogue

Powązki Cemetery

Powązki Cemetery, Żywiciel Group

Powązki Cemetery, Żywiciel Group

Pawiak Prison Gate

Pawiak Memorial Wall

I reached England a week after leaving the prisoner-of-war camp. Starved emotionally as well as physically, I began a period of readjustment—not just to freedom, but to the realization that I was finally severed from my family, friends, and home country. In spite of this realization, or perhaps because of it, I could not forget the events of the past five and a half years.

The nights were particularly bad, and I relived, over and over again, my experiences in Pawiak, the Ghetto, Szucha Avenue, and the Uprising. Only the period in the camp remained, mercifully, an unreal blur.

Excerpt from author's original handwritten diary

The doctors finally suggested that the best therapy would be for me to write down all that had happened, then put it aside and try to forget it. So, in the summer of 1945, I went to stay with a British family at their country house near Truro, Cornwall, in the southwest of England.

As I began to write (in Polish, for I spoke little English then), I found that dates, events, and names fell into place with awful precision, and I reconstructed several episodes with sketch maps. By the autumn, as my body began to accept proper meals again, my physical health gradually but steadily improved. Then I finished my manuscript, put it away, and finally began to enjoy emotional freedom too.

299

Trelissick, where author wrote original manuscript in the summer of 1945

Trelissick

The author—November 1945 (age sixteen)

Author's discharge papers, March 1946 (reason for discharge: under age)

It was fifteen years before I saw my family again, and by that time I was married, living in America, and working as an architect. The idea of sharing my wartime experiences with others did not occur to me, at least not until a few years ago during a visit to Warsaw; a friend told me then that most of the Freedom Fighters from Żoliborz were now resting at peace in Powązki Cemetery, having been moved from their wartime graves in the parks and gardens of the city. So, I went to Powązki to find Ludwik's grave, and the graves of my comrades from the Ninth Company Commandos.

I also visited the Szucha Avenue and Pawiak Museums, and the faithfully restored buildings, monuments, squares, and boulevards of Warsaw. I realized then that I owed it to all those who had suffered and perished to tell their story by telling mine. Moreover, I saw more clearly that the fight for freedom does not cease with the winning or losing of individual battles, but is timeless.

Robert Browning's words, from which I took the title of this book, are a tribute to all freedom fighters, past and present:

> **Good, to forgive;**
> **Best, to forget!**
> **Living, we fret!**
> **Dying, we live.**

The author today, in his doctoral robes from the Warsaw Institute of Technology

303

Illustration Credits

The author wishes to thank the following for permission to use illustrations in *Dying, We Live*.

Bundesarchiv: pp. 222, 240, and 241.

Central Archives of the Central Committee of the Polish United Workers Party: pp. 3 (top center), 11, 12, 16 (both), 17, 21, 27, 53, 54 (both), 55, 57, 74 (both), 75, 78, 79 (both), 80, 99, 107, 109, 111 (top), 112, 116 (top), 131, 133, 147, 157, 174, 183, 201, 216, 217, 218 (both), 219 (bottom), 225, 231 (top left), 231 (bottom left), 232, 245, 249, 259, 263, and 268 (both).

Historical Museum of the City of Warsaw: pp. 1 (left), 5 (bottom right), 6 (all), 15 (top right), 45, 47, 69, 98 (left), 101, 111 (bottom), 140 (all), 141, 212, 215, 219 (top left), 219 (top right), 224, 228, 229, 231 (top right), 231 (bottom right), 237, 239, 242, 243, 255 (all), 257, 260, 262, 266, and 267.

Jewish Historical Institute in Warsaw: pp. 5 (top right), 59, 61, 73, 89, 116 (bottom), 132, and 137.

Morag Kinnison: pp. 37, 138, and 303.

Przypkowski Collection: p. 1 (top) and 1 (right).

U. S. Department of the Army Photographic Library: pp. 274, 286 (both), 287, 291, and 299.

U. S. National Archives: pp. 15 (top left), 15 (bottom), 18 (all), 130, 134, 136, 142, 143, and 144 (all).

The remaining illustrations are from the author's private collection: frontispiece; pp. 2 (all), 3 (top left), 3 (top right), 3 (bottom), 4 (all), 5 (top left), 5 (bottom left), 5 (bottom center), 33, 34 (both), 35, 48, 77, 98 (right), 118, 119, 154, 164, 185, 188, 199, 219 (center left), 219 (center right), 295, 296 (both), 297, 298, 300 (both), 301, and 302.

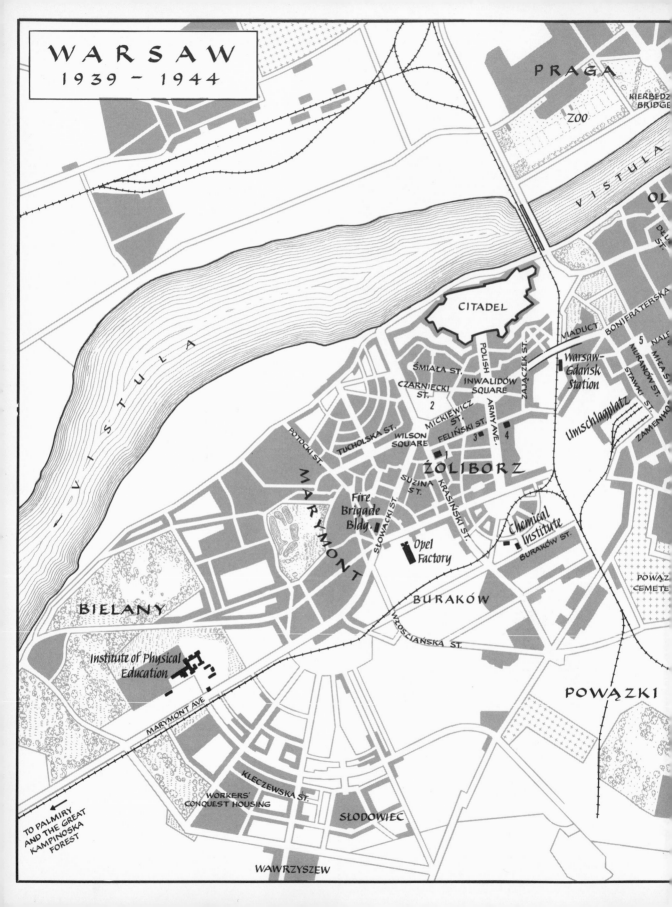